Unchain My Heart

Dogs Deserve Better Rescue Stories of Courage, Compassion, and Caring

EDITED BY

Tamira Ci Thayne and Dawn Ashby

Published by Crescent Renewal Resource
P.O. Box 23
Tipton, PA 16684

www.UnchainMyHeart.info
www.DogsDeserveBetter.org

Cover and book design by Tamira Thayne
Editor photo of Ms. Thayne by Christine Jaksy, dogdayart.com
Editor photo of Ms. Ashby by Darin Ashby
Cover photos, "Frankie" by Dick Cheatham

ISBN: 978-0-9842897-0-7

Printed in the United States of America

First Edition

We dedicate this book
to Area Rep Tamar Sherman,
a tireless advocate for chained dogs
who lost her life to breast cancer
in 2007.

And, to all dogs
still living chained
or penned today.

You deserve better.

Merry Christmas!
with love—
Layla
xo 2010

xo

2015

Table of Contents

❧

Foreword

BY TAMIRA CI THAYNE, DDB FOUNDER AND CEO

☙

"**T**his is all your fault, Tami," accused Pennsylvania area rep Kathy Slagle. "If it weren't for you, I'd still be getting my nails done and making sure I had the right shoes to go with my outfit."

"Well, it's not like I'm having any fun either," I retorted.

We both snickered, but it dawned on me that she was being serious. She *was* kinda' pissed.

Then it dawned on me that I was kinda' pissed too! Who's braniac idea was this anyway, birthing an organization that's taken over my being, my home, my every waking moment?

Kathy continued to lament, "I used to have time for relaxing, drinks with my friends, movies, dinner. Now it seems when I *do* get out, it's stolen time and I have to rush home to care for my dogs and foster dogs. And just so's you know, I blame you and this damn organization I dug up on the internet."

I suspect Kathy's not the only one—that most of our area reps have at one time or another stepped back and looked around bewilderedly, "Holy crap, where am I? What happened to my sanity, my ordinary life?"

I certainly have. But I know I wouldn't change it for all the manna in heaven. I suspect none of us has ever been as personally fulfilled as we are at the moment we see the light come back into a foster dog's eyes.

Yes, that moment.

Words do not exist that adequately describe how it feels to release a dog from its bondage into freedom, joy, and love.

I first see this dog with nothing, literally nothing but the dirt beneath his feet, trapped within a 20-foot radius, love to give but none to receive, and then one week later I watch the exact same dog crawl nonchalantly up onto the overstuffed chair after a long walk in the woods and fall asleep like he's been doing it his whole life.

But *I know he hasn't.*

It's that moment.

I love our Area Rep Program, and I adore our area reps. These women and men pour their hearts and souls into their rescue work. They educate, fundraise, build fences, and save dogs.

What you'll find in this book is but a tiny fraction of the stories we could tell; a tiny fraction of the joy, a tiny fraction of the heartbreak. I hope you'll appreciate reading them as much as we delight in bringing them to you.

As for Kathy, she was finally off to Italy the next week for much-needed couple time with her partner. I told her "Have a blast, and try to forgive me while you're over there."

She humpphed. "Forget that, there's no way I'm forgiving you."

Wow, she *was* kinda' pissed. Maybe the Italian wine will help.

Introduction

BY DAWN ASHBY, DIRECTOR OF ARS

(ARBITRARY & RANDOM SILLINESS, WHAT WERE *YOU* THINKING?)

℘

I've attended Animal Rights Conferences where Sea Shepherd's Captain Paul Watson was present. Admirers gathered 'round him to hang on his every word as he told tales from the high seas, such as the one about the time he looked into the eye of a giant whale he was protecting and felt the bonding of spirit.

So I tried that myself. I grabbed a random person walking by the DDB booth and proclaimed, "I once looked in the eyes of a chained Min Pin…" but that's as far as I got before my captive audience pushed me away, wild-eyed, and ran to find the security guard. I don't know why Captain Paul gets notoriety while I just get another restraining order filed against me. Tami says it's his uniform. I think it's the big boat and the fact that he sometimes blows things up. (Cool!)

Another time, while in charge of the DDB booth, a woman walked up to me and said, "You are my hero!" I thought, "*Finally*, someone gets me!"

But then she went on to say, "I admire you for going to jail for that dying chained dog…" and I realized she must not have known what Tami looked like and assumed I was Tami minding the booth. She asked me to autograph her copy of *Scream Like Banshee*, yeah, by Tamira Ci Thayne.

I really wanted to write in her book. I yearned to bleed on a page, "Nancy, you are King Kong squashing my heart in your hairy hand like an over-ripe banana." But of course I didn't. Not because I'm not Tami and it would be morally wrong to mislead this woman, but because gorillas have opposable thumbs and I wasn't sure if I should refer to them as having hands or paws, plus I wasn't confident that my metaphor was proportionately correct. I mean King Kong has some pretty big hands, if that is in fact what they are, so an over-ripe banana would be a little speck in comparison…. and last… I thought…well I would sort of be putting a metaphor and simile in the same sentence and I don't even know if that's legal…

So instead, I did the decent thing and tried to be almost honest and signed the book, "Dear Nancy, I HATE YOU. Sincerely, Tamira Ci Thayne."

As Nancy walked away she must have overheard someone say Tami's name because I saw her gaze turn to a crowd surrounding the real Tamira Ci Thayne. A look of uncertainty crossed Nancy's face as she stopped and opened her book to look for the autographed entry, then turned an accusing glare in my direction. I grabbed another copy, plopped it over Tami's shoulder, and whispered in her ear "Sign this To Nancy."

I had to rely on my spy training that no one knows about because its top secret (oops!) to pull off what we call in the Business, "The Ol' Switcherooski." I calculatedly and physically ran into the woman, knocked the book from her hands, and switched the copies before she could even yell, "Help, she's a maniac!" Cleverly, I secured the original copy I had signed, paid for it back at the booth (I'm honest like that), and then tossed it into my bag with the rest of the forgeries.

All that just to be noticed. Sigh.

I am confident that every representative of Dogs Deserve Better has a story to tell, and nothing like this one. That's why I twisted Tami's arm to put this book together. Dogs Deserve Better representatives no longer have to impersonate Tami or accost strangers in order to share their rescue stories. *Unchain My Heart* is their book, it's our book.

As DDB area reps we almost never—except on Thursdays—liberate chained or penned dogs for praise, fame, or reward. A simple, sloppy wet lick is all the reward we need. Yet, I've heard some amazing tales from many of our reps and I'm excited about getting them in print for you, the reader, because these stories deserve to have an audience, and these dogs deserve to have a voice.

Kick off your shoes and snuggle up with your favorite furry friend and we'll share with you just a few of our rescue adventures…all with guaranteed happy endings.

But one final warning: Neither Dogs Deserve Better nor the editors, Tamira Ci Thayne and Dawn Ashby, can be held liable for any DDB area rep who waylays you, wrestles this book from your grip, turns to the page where his or her story is told, and autographs it as he or she likes.

Disclaimer: Though I confess most of what I just told you is arbitrary silliness and never happened, I really am a highly trained top-secret spy.

Donte:
Breaking Chains and Breaking Curses

BY SHARI STRADER, DDB NORTH CAROLINA REP

℘

Donte watched silently, day after day, from his place on a chain in the yard next door while we installed a fence for his neighbor, Tiger. When we finished Tiger's fence we knew we had to help Donte too. As I drew near, he exhibited all the signs of a chained backyard dog—he was afraid, territorial, and appeared vicious; but then I knelt down and the kiss-fest began.

He wasn't a bad dog—he just needed off the chain and a little love.

When I approached the guardians, I quickly found they didn't speak a word of English. Inconvenient. Not to be deterred, I set out to learn all the pertinent Spanish words I would need to help Donte. Fortunately, when I returned to talk to them, they had a bilingual friend available, and believe it or not, Donte was released to Dogs Deserve Better!

Donte was a big dog, a Great Dane mix who just loved to jump—mostly straight up in the air like a kangaroo. He didn't know how to walk on a leash, didn't have any social skills whatsoever, wanted nothing but to play, and hadn't a clue how big he really was. These traits made things interesting trying to wrangle him into the car to head to the vet; I'm hoping no one was watching, but if they were, they had quite the laugh at our expense!

At the vet's office we found signs of a previously embedded collar or chain, and the chain currently around his neck was so tight it nearly had to be cut off. He also had scars and sores on his leg from the chain wrapping around and digging into it. Luckily, despite these minor health issues, he was still a young, healthy dog.

I then faced my next hurdle: where to take this huge, 90-pound jumping-straight-up-in-the-air dog. I could not find a foster home but luckily—or so I thought at the time—found a kennel that gave a great discount for rescue dogs. After checking it out, I decided to board him there until a forever or foster home could be found. I would go over daily to walk and socialize him, and continue my search for something more permanent, a home setting to get started on his housetraining.

Right off the bat he displayed aggression toward the owner of the kennel, but not the woman, just the man. I realized he'd probably been abused by a man, and would need to be placed in a home with a very mild-mannered man or no men at all.

While at the kennel, Donte's leg was healing from the chain injuries nicely, but then he developed a new sore on his healthy leg, one that hadn't been there before. After several visits to different vets we discovered the origin of his new sore. He had been bitten on his foot by a poisonous spider . . . a brown recluse!

We acted quickly to remove him from the spider-infested kennel and he had to be hospitalized for his bite. His foot needed constant care—wet to dry bandages, antibiotics, cleanings. Finally, he was ready to be placed in a temporary foster home which I'd found through numerous internet postings and cross-postings, and I was hoping that soon we'd be on a good path to adoption for this poor dog.

As luck would have it, at the new foster home Donte began tearing the bandages off his foot. They didn't make an e-collar big enough to keep him from being able to stick his long legs in and get to the bandages. We'd put one on and an hour later we'd find small pieces of the tell-tale white cloth all about the yard and house.

I never found big sections of bandages, but just assumed he had torn them to shreds. Soon after, he began getting really sick so back to the vet we went. With the help of x-rays the mystery of the missing bandages was solved—the rest of Dontes bandages were, drumroll please . . . in his stomach!

Donte had to have major abdominal surgery to remove the bandages, plus several more weeks of hospitalization. Finally, a few weeks later, Donte's foot and stomach were both on the mend and I was starting to see light at the end of our tunnel. That boy was a survivor, I'll give him that!

I may have been frazzled and close to death from stress overload, but Donte somehow came through it all with a light in his eyes and a cheery disposition, always happy to see me and all his new friends.

One night while Donte was still at the vet hospital, someone dumped two dogs over the fence, a male and a female. If you are a person who believes that things happen for a reason, you too will believe that Donte's path, difficult as it may have been, led him to where he was supposed to be! For one of the abandoned dogs, the female, and Donte fell madly in love. They were inseparable, constant companions.

I began to worry about separating them once Donte was adopted, but I didn't have to worry for long. One of the clients of the vet saw Donte and his girlfriend, fell in love with the duo, and adopted them both into their family.

I think Donte was cursed with a run of bad luck, then Lady Luck came along and broke the spell, propelling him to the happiness he'd never known.

Love is said to be a divine magical power which connects two hearts together, the strongest power of all.

While Donte's success story was long, tumultuous, and downright painful for both of us, in the end the success was even sweeter for all the difficulties we overcame.

I sometimes wonder how he'd be now if our paths had not crossed. Would he still be chained? Would he even be alive?

One thing *is* for sure—this time it was not the journey but the destination that mattered most. And Donte has arrived. Finally, he's living the life he deserves.

Donte, with his new family, and his doggie girlfriend

Eau de Dog
or "I Draw Dog Talk"

BY TAMIRA CI THAYNE, DOGS DESERVE BETTER FOUNDER

℘

Tami holding Foo Foo Cuddly Poops

I don't know what it is. Maybe it happens to you too. I often look down at my clothing to see if I'm wearing DDB pins or attire that would signal 'dog lady' and start people around me to talkin' 'bout dogs. But most of the time it's just me, wearing simple jeans, simple shirt, and touting around my over-sized red purse and iPhone.

Nothing to give me away as "The Dog Thief, Blair County, Pennsylvania, hold-on to your dogs, cause she's a headin' your way."

Yet, everywhere I go, whether it be fancy four-star restaurant (yeah, I go there) or the local convenience store, I'm surrounded with dog talk, filling the airwaves and wafting through the ether.

"I took my dog to the groomer yesterday..."
"My dog just doesn't like this new food..."
"We had to put our dog to sleep last week..."

I think I must have Eau de Dog oozing from my every pore or something.

On this occasion I happen to take my son to a local gas station for a soda when I overhear one girl telling another about two starving Shepherds in her neighborhood. The house is pretty much abandoned, and they are so hungry they are killing local critters and eating them.

My ears perk up, and against my preference for an uneventful Saturday evening, my feet propel me toward her. "I'm sorry to interrupt," I say, "but are these dogs chained outside?"

She replies, "Yes, they are—they're skinny, and the one is downright scary. He broke free and backed me into a corner and I thought he was going to attack me."

I quickly ask for directions, run home, grab my camera, food, and water, and I'm back out the door to get there before darkness hits.

I can't see the dogs from the road, but I know the house as soon as I see it. Trash everywhere, abandoned cars, piles upon piles of junk and broken down equipment, tires, and machinery. "Yep, this is it," I say to myself even before I hear the dogs barking.

I recognize the trademark signs of many a dog-chainer: the dog is chained outside amidst the wreckage, just another piece of the abandoned garbage marking the property.

I quickly scan the cars scattered about the yard to see if any of them have been driven recently. The car sitting at the end of the driveway looks fairly new, and still has keys in the ignition. I'm think-ing someone must be living here, then, despite the tip to the contrary and the obviously disgusting appearance of the place. I cautiously walk up the driveway and head straight to the door to knock.

The local humane officer—and I use the term loosely—is always quick to tell me to mind my P's and Q's and not to trespass onto other peoples' property. However, it's perfectly legal to go up to anyone's door, knock, and attempt to speak to them—Jehovah's Witnesses do it all the time!

So I make my way through the rubble, climb the broken-down stairs, weave through the old clothes, hamster cage, and kitchen table on the porch, and knock on the front door. I knock again. No answer.

Two cats are meowing and following me as I traverse, asking for food and water too, and I talk to them in soothing tones, stooping to give them a pet, a scratch on the ear, and some dog food. I don't have any cat food with me, but I figure beggar kitties are not in a position to be chooser kitties. I figure right, and they tuck in for perhaps the first full meal they've had in awhile.

I can immediately see and hear the first Shepherd, but I also hear the other Shepherd off to the left, and I see a third black dog, a bor-der collie mix, who is eyeing me up over to the right. I stop and knock at the side door, which is standing partially open, but am certainly not stupid enough to attempt to enter the home.

No, I don't believe anyone lives here. Too trashed for at least the majority of humankind to deal with.

I move further up the hill toward the dogs, getting a sense of the situation, when I spot a blur of white movement coming from straight ahead behind some piles of boards. I'm filming now, and as I walk toward the movement I quickly ascertain that it's actually a little white dog. I'm shocked and horrified when I take in her condition.

Her eyes cannot see, and her ears cannot hear. She is white, but matted, filthy white, and with blue eyes, but one is covered by a cataract and the other is red instead of blue. She looks demonic.

I call to her repeatedly before realizing that she can't hear me, and my heart is just broken for her. She is not chained, but rather in a little penned area, and has only a dog crate for a home. I go inside to meet her, and she initially smells me and comes toward me gratefully before realizing she doesn't know me and becoming scared.

She then growls and barks in some pitiful attempt to scare me off, running into her crate for what little protection it can offer. She is shaking her head incessantly, and I can tell that she has a major ear infection in addition to her obvious sight problems.

She's truly one of the most wretched creatures I've ever seen.

Chained to the left of the white dog's area resides the first Shepherd, who must be the aggressive male, because I'm pretty sure he wants to tear me limb from limb.

I'm embarrassed to admit I'm shaking from head to toe; since the attempted homicide on my person by the previously-chained Chow Chow, I can't help but react with fear when I perceive aggressive behavior in a dog. I hope someday to get over it, but for now I just muddle along doing my best in spite of those fears.

I pass the scary Shepherd and head between the bushes and an old camping trailer to the other Shepherd. This Shepherd must be the female, because she's behaving the polar opposite of the male. She's totally submissive, ears flattened to her head, and lowering herself closer to the ground. She is heartbreakingly, adorably, running back and forth with her metal pot in her mouth, begging me, "Please give me food, please give me water. I can't last out here much longer like this!"

I'm not afraid of this one at all, and I immediately give her some of the water I've brought in a gallon jug, as well as some of the food

I've packed. Despite her emaciated state, she's not interested in the food, but instead drinks and drinks the water like she hasn't had it in weeks.

I have a harder time giving the male water because he lunges at me, snapping and barking when I come near, but I do manage to get the bowl down and get myself back out of the way before he gets to me. God forbid he should break free at this particular moment! That would not be good for me.

I then focus again on the little foo foo dog, putting some food on the ground for her, cleaning the filthy water from her dish, and pouring her some fresh water. I put everything near her so she can find it, and she devours the food from the ground, looking for more.

The border collie is the only one who appears to be in decent shape, is even overweight, and I wonder if he's a new addition to the menagerie of neglected creatures on this property. There seems to be no other explanation for the differences in body condition.

With everyone fed and watered, I can feel safe in going home to consider what to do about the situation. No one is in immediate danger of death, but something must be done ASAP for these dogs.

I post photos of the three dogs on my Facebook page, and video of the female Shepherd running with her dish and begging for water and food. I lament the fact that there's no reliable help to be had for these dogs, especially on a holiday weekend.

In the Doogie case, I did what needed to be done because authorities wouldn't—and I got arrested—but at least the dog survived, got the vet help he needed, and lived another 5-1/2 months, inside, with a home and family. Just two weeks prior to this case, I investigated a case of two severely neglected St. Bernards in Johnstown, Pennsylvania, and this time I tried it by the book.

A gravely-ill St. Bernard Thayne tried to help

It was evening, and I knew there would be no getting ahold of the Cambria County Humane Society at that time...it's hard enough between 9-5. So I put a call into the local police department—which both the DA and the judge told me I should have done in the Doogie case—even though I knew full well what the outcome would be.

The officer I spoke to on the phone, who never would tell me his name, said they'd investigate "as time permits." I said, "What does that mean? I don't understand what that means—an hour, three days, what?" He got very nasty with me, telling me he didn't know when it would be and hung up on me.

The tipsters and I were discussing how to proceed when an officer, apparently the police chief or some such, pulled up in an police SUV. He told us to go on home, not to go back on the property, and he'd call the dog warden in the morning and 'do it the right way.' I explained to him that the dog warden doesn't do cruelty, but only checks for license and rabies, and he'd need the Cambria County humane officer for this case if he's refusing to investigate it himself. He was surprised, and didn't even KNOW there *was* a humane officer in Cambria County! That tells you how seriously animal cruelty is taken here in Pennsylvania.

I got up early the next morning and drove back up there only to find that all three dogs on the property were gone. It was obvious that the cop tipped off the dogs' guardian, who went out there, removed the dogs, and 'did away' with the worst one, the one who really needed immediate veterinary care.

That's how it ends when you do it the legal way here in Pennsylvania.

So now here I am on Facebook, lamenting and brainstorming with my friends about the current case and the four needy dogs, when I get a message from Facebook friend Jodi Goldberg, asking what county the dogs are in. Seems that her organization, the Pennsylvania SPCA, is badged in more and more counties these days, and if it's a county they are badged in they will send someone out the next day to take a look at the situation! Could there be a spark of hope igniting within me for these dogs?

I know if it's my county, Blair, the dogs are just as screwed as Doogie and I were. It's close, though...I look at a map, and see that both Huntingdon and Centre County are right in the same vicinity, so there's a good chance the PSCPA can help.

The next day I again bring the dogs food and water, and investigate the address to figure out in which county the residence lies.

This time the male Shepherd isn't as aggressive with me, and I believe there's a chance to rehabilitate him. I hope to find someone who specializes in working with this kind of aggression in Shepherds. Both Shepherds appear purebred, a plus for him, as Shepherds are known to be highly trainable dogs and very good listeners.

I spend more time with the dog Brynnan and I have named Foo Foo Cuddly Poops—from the Nickelodeon show The Last Airbender—because we always giggle when we hear them say it in the show. We've been waiting for awhile to name a dog Foo Foo Cuddly Poops, but we get mostly big dogs—it just wouldn't work for them. We decide this sweet little girl will work beautifully!

She's truly a pitiful wretch, not only is she blind and deaf, but she is COVERED in fleas from head to toe, her ears are full of black caked 'gunk', and her fur is matted all the way to her little body. I try to videotape her ear condition, but just me pulling her ear back for the camera makes her shriek with pain. I feel awful that I hurt her, and I try to soothe her with gentle petting strokes to let her know I'm here for her. I promise I will get her out as soon as possible.

She was obviously a lap dog in the past, and I can't imagine the horror of finding yourself not only unable to see or hear, but suddenly left outside, alone and vulnerable, in pain and not understanding how or why this happened.

Thank Dog it's just starting to get a fall chill to the air, and the days are still plenty warm enough, without being sweltering, that at least I didn't have to worry about her freezing.

It's obvious to me that no one has been here since yesterday.

Everything remains the same as the day before; I sense an eery, still feeling to the air.

I get the address from the mailbox, and ascertain that it is indeed Centre County: good news for these dogs. I know that the PSPCA is badged in this county, and if they hold true to their word, something may actually be done for these dogs! And quickly!

I call Jodi and provide her with the county name and address when I get home. That afternoon, the PSPCA dispatches someone to go out there—on a weekend! On Labor Day weekend, no less! I'm floored.

They find sufficient evidence of abuse to go for a warrant, which they successfully obtain on Sunday morning. They bring two trucks all the way over from Philadelphia, and, as luck would have it (in a good way this time), when they get there the caretaker is on the premises. They convince him to sign over all four dogs, a VERY positive event, and they still plan to file abuse charges against him.

Wow!

Wow! Now that's how it's done, America!

The dogs must go to Philadelphia to be checked out for the cruelty case and documented by their veterinarian. After that, they will release them to me and Dogs Deserve Better's foster program, but I have to get down there quickly—turns out that while the PSPCA has a great cruelty program, dogs who don't get moved into foster care or other rescue groups still stand a very good chance of going down.

I drive the four hours with my partner, Joe, and we pick up three of the four dogs: Vivian, the female Shepherd, Foo Foo Cuddly Poops, the blind/deaf Spitz-Pom mix, and Sampson, a Border Collie mix.

I visit the male Shepherd while I'm there, and he's stuck in a crate from which he doesn't get relief because he's barking and snapping aggressively at anyone who comes near him. Jodi and I pledge to look for trainers to help him; we both find a few good leads in the next two days, but we are too late. He goes down that Wednesday.

I will never know if he could have/would have/should have been rehabilitated, but I can't help but believe he deserved that chance, and am saddened that he didn't get it.

Foo Foo Cuddly Poops explores the yard after her grooming

I cling to the three successes I still house in my home. Foo Foo has made a dramatic turnaround in the past month, and is a different dog. After I chop-chopped her fur to remove some of the more obvious mats, she went to a groomer where it was done right (no charge—thank you, Linda!), and her ears are much improved.

She is scheduled to fly out on the Pilots for Paws program to a rescue in Tennessee, but the vet grounds her from flying because her mouth is in horrible shape, and he says it's giving her a lot of pain. He removes 16 teeth that afternoon, and by the next day she's already playing and cuddling.

Fate must have finally brought Foo Foo some good news, because the next evening a former adopter (and another Facebook friend) stops by with some blanket beds she's made for the dogs. She asks to meet Foo Foo. She—of course, how could you not—falls in love with the little darling, goes home to discuss adoption with her husband, and calls back to arrange getting her on Saturday!

Now Foo Foo will again know the home of her dreams...sitting on a lap or on the couch with her loved ones, being cuddled, pampered, and caressed the way she has always deserved to be.

Sampson is now fixed and working on his housetraining. He's a bit difficult to train, not only because he's male and overly fond of lifting his leg, but also because he doesn't get along with the other male dogs in the house, so has to be kept separated.

He spends much of his time in our inside/outside homemade crate system or in the office downstairs with Kim and Vivian.

Sampson poses for his Petfinder picture

What is this crate system, you ask, since if you're fostering you may want to try this at home? Using our engineering genius (eh-hem), we connected two large crates, giving the foster dog(s) extra room, and set it up directly in front of the doggie door in our office. So, Sampson—or whoever is in need of this system due to aggression, separation anxiety, destructive tendancies, or housetraining issues— can be inside as part of the pack, but not able to get to anyone or anything he might want to mess with.

Whenever he wants to go outside to potty or sniff around and get exercise, he just jaunts out through the doggie door. There's plenty of room for two-three dogs if they all get along and need to be safely contained yet still have access to the fenced yard.

Vivian is still skinny, despite being fed two meals a day, and we are testing and investigating what could be the root of the problem. I've started putting enzymes into her food, in case she has EPI—Endocrine Pancreatic Insuffiency (inability to digest her food) as many Shepherds do. I know I could easily rehome her—many people want purebred female Shepherds—but as of right now my daughter Brynnan is in love with her and begging to keep her here as part of our family.

Whether she stays with us or finds another loving, forever home—after she's spayed and gained some weight—remains to be seen. Regardless, three of four of these babies are now safe, vetted, de-fleaed, heartworm-treated, and either looking for or have already found loving, forever homes.

Really, not a bad outcome for a simple trip to the gas station for soda . . . a little Eau de Dog went a long way for this trio of mistreated pups.

Zoey
The Keep 'er

BY TAMMI KINMAN RUPPERT, DDB KENTUCKY REP

ℊ

I became aware of Zoey late last year when contacted by a DDB volunteer who also helped at a local shelter. She said there was a dog due to be put down and she knew the dog had been chained outside her entire life. Her caregiver had dropped her off, now she was going from life on a chain directly to her death in the shelter. "Could you do anything?" she asked. It was Friday; the dog was to be put down Monday. I told her the truth, I would try my best, and then I began praying.

I had to take one of my own dogs to our vet that Friday, and as I was paying the bill, another woman walked in and we started chatting at the counter. I always try to work Dogs Deserve Better into a conversation whenever possible, especially places that I find people with pets. I told the woman I was trying to save a dog from euthanasia and searching for a temporary foster home for her. She took my number and said she would see what she could do. Later that day she called me. She had the number of a good person who might be willing to foster Zoey.

I called the number and was invited over for a quick home visit. The family agreed they would take the dog in for a night and try her out on a sleepover basis. I figured this bought me one day, a day that could save Zoey's life. If it didn't work out, I'd cross that bridge when I came to it. I was able to pick her up from the shelter that Monday, on the day she was to be killed.

She went to her foster home on Monday and the next day, I received a call from her foster family saying, "We love her, and we'll keep her." That was easy, almost too easy. Zoey got to start her new life in a great foster home where she was loved, pampered, even taken to work everyday with her foster parents. Each time I spoke with her foster parents, I would ask if they were ready for me to list her for adoption. The answer was always the same, "No Way!" They weren't ready to give her up yet, but they weren't interested in adopting her themselves either.

This continued for several months. Then I received a troubling phone call. It was Zoey's foster mom, "Come and get her. I don't want her anymore."

Something must have gone terribly wrong, but I was left in the dark. I had my suspicions about a combination of heath issues and other problems in the family that would prevent them from keeping Zoey. "Here we go again," I thought, "me with Zoey, and nowhere for her to go." If only her foster parents would have been cooperative when I wanted to post her for adoption she may have been in her forever home already.

I sent out an emergency e-mail requesting help from my colleagues at DDB. A volunteer came through for Zoey. A real estate agent, she had recently sold a home to a young doctor and his wife who had relocated from Virginia. The couple was open to fostering Zoey!

I was introduced to them and then I stopped by for a home check.

They were thrilled when they met Zoey and she certainly seemed delighted with them. Their new home had a large back yard in a neighborhood filled with families and dogs, dogs living INSIDE where they belong. Zoey went up for adoption right away and quite a few inquiries came in for her. I called to tell her foster family there were potential adopters interested in Zoey and was met with the same problem as before. The foster family was not ready to let her go.

This time was slightly different, however. The family, once again, asked, "Can we keep her?" But this time they didn't mean keep her as a prolonged foster home, they meant as Zoey's forever home!

I told them nothing would make me happier. Zoey was adopted into her forever family, but that was not the end of the good news. Zoey's new parents requested they remain a foster home and look after other dogs for Dogs Deserve Better.

That's how Zoey came to have a new playmate. Woody, an 8-year-old rescued Chihuahua is being fostered and living temporarily with Zoey and her family while he waits for his forever adoptive family. How does Zoey feel about this arrangement? She's just a happy-go-lucky girl, seemingly unfazed by her rough start and near death experience. Now she's not only enjoying her life to the fullest, but she's made room for other dogs in need to stay with her until they find homes of their own.

Tree Hugger's
Twelve-Dog Rescue

BY DAWN ASHBY, DDB ILLINOIS REP

ß

Snowball, one of 12 dogs rescued in one week by Ashby

"**O**oph!" It's the sound I make when I smack face first into an inanimate object—current said object being a tree. In case you're wondering, this isn't the first time I've heard myself make the sound, *"Ooph!"*

The first time it happened was after Hurricane Katrina, when I assisted at a make-shift shelter in Mississippi. I volunteered to walk a Pit Bull who by the looks of him was apparently raised on steroids. His human mom left him in our care while she went back to Louisiana to salvage some of her belongings.

Since I was the first one brave enough to walk him, I followed his mom's instructions and attached two reinforced leads to both of the

21

collars he wore. As soon as I opened the kennel door the scene went something like this, *"Whoaaaah! Ooph!"*

He was out the door and headed to the parking lot, the last place he saw his mom before she left him. I slammed face first into a metal beam holding up the ceiling and held on for dear life. Incidentally, after this, the rescue I was volunteering for decided two people must accompany all dogs during a walk. Apparently I'm the person rules are made for.

"Ooph!"

This time, I cling to the tree with both legs and my left arm, giving myself yet another reason to be called a tree hugger. My right arm is using all its concentration to remind my right hand, "Don't let go!"

I'm just like Jack Dawson and Rose DeWitt Bukater after the sinking of the Titanic, floating in the icy ocean, "Don't let go! You can never let go!" Only instead of Leonardo Dicaprio's icy fingers I am gripping a strained-to-the-limit dog leash at the end of which is a Great Pyrenees named Snowball.

If you've ever let go of a leash attached to a dog who's been just-released from the chain you'll understand that it's much easier to live life with one arm longer than the other than to try to catch a dog who's discovered absolute freedom. The phrase "A Snowball's chance in hell" comes to mind, but I'll spare you the pun.

Now my problem is figuring out how to get my aching body, the tree and the dog back to my truck. Since the tree isn't going anywhere, I solve the problem by encouraging one of two large men standing and laughing at me to bring my truck here. "Keys are in the ignition!" I call out, and finally manage to successfully maneuver Snowball directly inside the cab.

When his caregiver signs the surrender contract stating, "I will not chain or pen dogs on my property" he asks what he owes me for taking Snowball off his hands. Besides reconstructive surgery on my face I can think of nothing. Like Snowball, I just want to escape this place.

I drive Snowball to the vet; fortunately the dog is not as keyed up to leave the truck cab as he was to leave his life chained inside a garage. At the vet's office I check the scale three times before asking Doc to come into the reception area, "Is your scale working?" I ask.

I just can't believe this enormous Great Pyrenees who pulled me around the yard is weighing in at only 73 pounds! Doc has to feel under Snowball's thick, matted, dingy-white coat to discover the bag of bones that is all there is to poor Snowball.

Snowball is number eleven of twelve rescued chained dogs this week for me; a busy week even by my standards. The dogs range in size from a small, chained Miniature Pinscher named Snickers (people will chain anything they can get a collar on) to Snowball, the large Great Pyrenees.

At this moment, all twelve dogs are joining me on a transport to various foster and adoptive homes in and around Chicago. Among the other dogs on the transport is Sophie, a sweet white Maltese who had to be taken off the adoption page after ten minutes due to an overwhelming number of calls—proving that one man's chained/

penned lawn ornament is another man's treasure—and Faith, who was left behind, chained in a yard, when her caregiver's moved.

Faith, in her yard and awaiting rescue

Faith's story and subsequent adoption success even made the Chicago Tribune with the news editor noting, "This is no way to treat man's best friend." Amen, so glad you see it our way!

Today I'm accompanied on the transport by Erin, a woman who read an article about me in the newspaper and told her husband, "This woman Dawn is my hero." *Hero* is how people describe me before actually meeting me in person; after that my status diminishes to something along the lines of "crazy dog lady who runs into trees."

I borrow my parent's van to fit all twelve dogs. I accomplish this by explaining to them, in a mumbly voice, that I am transporting "a coupla' dogs." My parents are old—my dad already suffered one stroke—and if I were to admit to twelve dogs riding in their vehicle there's a good chance I'd be putting them both into cardiac arrest. I'll clean the interior extra well to cover my tracks, and they'll never be the wiser (unless they read this story, of course).

Wow! Just think: one woman rescues twelve chained dogs, moves them in a single transport—with only one minor incident (her face colliding with a tree)—and all grab up great new families and inside homes. A grateful heart quickly heals a swollen nose.

One By One,
They Passed Him By

BY PAULINE LARSEN, DDB IOWA REP

℘

Homeless, hungry, and very tired, Jackson plodded along the highway. He had been traveling quite a while and his steps grew slower and slower. His fur was matted and his feet sore. It was a hot, muggy day and he needed a drink. Cars whizzed beside him, and one by one they passed him by. Just when all seemed hopeless, a car stopped and a Rescue Angel called to him.

He mustered up his last bit of energy to wag his tail and hobbled to the car. Realizing the dog needed immediate care the woman turned the car around and headed to the vet where they clipped off his dirty matted fur, cleaned him up, and checked him over. The vet recognized the dog and sadly told how the dog's caregivers really weren't "dog people."

Because of normal dog activities like barking, chewing, and digging he was soon left chained in the yard away from the house so he wouldn't bother the humans. It was the children's responsibility to feed and care for him and they often forgot. The only visits to the vet were when he became so flea-infested that he developed sores. The vet had suggested they should perhaps re-home him, but they just shrugged and said, "He's just a dog. He does fine where he is."

Jackson's rescuer brought him to TLC Canine Center where fresh water, food, and a soft cushy bed awaited him, and then resolved to find out who had neglected the poor fellow for so long.

Only a few days later she identified the family and stopped to visit them. They could not understand her concern over "just a dog."

They had decided he was merely a bother and the kids really wanted a puppy, so they unlocked the log chain, put him in the back of the pickup, drove three miles from home, and then stopped and left him by the side of the road. When the Rescue Angel told them that animal abandonment was against the law, the man just shrugged, smiled, and asked if she wanted to see the new puppy.

℘

Jackson has quickly become a favorite at the center. He obviously led a tough life and certainly doesn't qualify as a show dog. He isn't particularly handsome—he's missing some teeth, and his few remaining ones are somewhat crooked, giving him a mischievous-looking grin.

He intently "listens" to you; although he is totally deaf. When he lays his head on your lap your heart just melts. His demands are few and what a comforting companion this dignified old guy would be if given half a chance.

Jackson is in a fog most of the time, but it's a happy fog….he loves to snuggle, he loves his cozy den, and always cleans his dinner plate. On his good days, he's eager to go for a walk. Jackson is special and he will be honored and loved for the rest of his days.

One by One, They Pass Me By (for Jackson):

One by one they pass me by. "Too old" "Too worn" "Too broken" they sigh.

"Way past his time, we want a puppy who'll run and play"

They shake their heads slowly and go on their way.

A little old man, arthritic and sore; it seems I'm not wanted anymore.

I once had a home; I once had a bed, a place that was warm and where
    I was fed.

Now my muzzle is gray, and my eyes slowly fail. Who wants a dog so old
    and so frail?

My family decided I didn't belong; they wanted a pup, was that so wrong?

Whatever excuse they made in their head can't justify how they left me
    for dead.

Now I sit here day after day, while the young ones get adopted away.

TLC loves me, gives me food and a bed, even a pillow for my poor tired head.

We snuggle and play and some day they say, someone will come and take
    me away.

I would promise to return all the love I can give, to someone, for as long as
    I live.

If only they wouldn't, just pass me by.

Touched
By an Angel

BY CHRISTINE HAVENS, DDB GEORGIA REP

❦

An Angel touched me one August evening in Canton, Georgia. I was taking pictures for my photography class when I heard a dog barking. As I peered into a backyard I saw nothing out of the ordinary. I began to turn away when, like an apparition, Angel appeared. She'd moved in and out of my view a few times, before I noticed her movement was restricted. To find a dog on a chain in Canton wasn't much of a surprise, so I was able to quickly ascertain her dilemma. Cautiously I ambled up to her and met the sweetest Angel.

A young girl came bouncing around the house. "Is she your dog?" I inquired as I looked up from Angel's pleading eyes.

She replied, "Yes," so I took the opportunity to inform her about

Dogs Deserve Better and the work we do. The girl, Juana, an eighth grader, was very willing, listened intently, and I concluded she already knew Angel deserved better.

When I first encountered Angel she was on a three-foot chain attached to a stake in the ground. The chain was so tight around her neck I couldn't even get a finger under it. I asked Juana to loosen the chain. I told her about DDB's fencing opportunities and spoke about proper training to get Angel to calm down. I said I would have her spayed for free so maybe we could get her back in the house for good. Juana agreed that this was a great idea.

Juana's family is from Guatamala and lives way below the poverty line. They love animals and only had Angel chained because the neighbors didn't like her running around in their yard. Their neighbors don't like dogs, are unruly, and fairly often drunk, which makes Juana afraid that they will someday hurt Angel.

I brought Juana's family a halter and leash. We were able to construct a fence and have Angel spayed as I worked on signing her up for obedience classes. As a representative for Dogs Deserve Better I feel great that I am able to make life better for both pets and their people. I feel like a guardian angel for a dog named Angel as well as Juana, a young girl from Guatemala who will now grow up with her best friend as part of her family. Thanks to Dogs Deserve Better all of our hearts have been "Touched by an Angel."

Juana, with the dogs in their new fenced yard.

Amy,
aka The Monkey Dog

BY MARIE BELANGER, DDB INDIANA REP & NATIONAL REP COORDINATOR

ℬ

Amy is a Beagle/Hound mix who was adopted from an Indiana humane society by an elderly couple. They did everything right for her . . . took her to the vet for a checkup and vaccines and then very soon after, took her in to be spayed. Amy was adored by the gentleman in the home, in fact, she was his best friend. She went places with him and she slept beside him on the sofa. Then, he passed away of a heart attack and Amy sorely grieved his passing.

The woman was not so fond of Amy and soon she was not allowed to even come inside the home anymore. At this point it was discovered that even though Amy looks like 100% dog, she is apparently part monkey. She can scale a 6" chain link fence with ease, using her toes just like fingers; this made it very difficult for the woman to contain her. So she ended up tethered to a little doghouse out in the middle of the fenced yard.

Soon the man's wife passed away too, and now the son was in possession of the home and poor Amy. He didn't live there, but two blocks down the street and came by daily to feed and water her. When I got the call from someone in her neighborhood seeking help for the situation and her, I immediately drove over to meet Amy, and found her to be beyond eager for some love and attention.

After meeting Amy I decided to drive down to the son's house and find out about her. At first he was quite defensive about the situation but after I explained to him that I was just there to offer him a free service and was not accusing him of anything, he agreed to drive back to where Amy was and let me in the fence to play with her. She was so starved for attention!

After a couple days of me going down to play with her, he agreed to sign her over to me so I could find her a new home. Well, that was just fine with me except for one little glitch; I had nowhere for her to go. Foster homes at this point were bursting at the seams and my two female German Shepherds weren't going to have any part of me bringing another dog into our tiny home. My next step taught me a very valuable lesson.

I called the original complaintants and gave them the good news and the bad news. Amy had been released to Dogs Deserve Better— Yay!—and I had nowhere to take her. I told them to get on the phone and call everyone they knew and ask if they would either like to adopt Amy or could give her a comfy foster home until I could place her with a new family.

To my surprise, they called me back in just one day; they had found a wonderful lady out in the country who was willing to foster Amy for me!

I now incorporate this method into every rescue call I get, and many times the very people who are concerned about the chained dog are instrumental in finding a foster or forever home.

After talking to the potential foster home and making her aware that Amy is very good at disguising the fact that she is part monkey, she still agreed to take her in. I posted Amy everywhere I could to find her a forever home but to no avail (most people who are looking for a dog are not interested in taking in a monkey).

Two months later Amy's foster mom called and notified me that her entire family had to pick up and leave for quite some time and I needed to find a place for Amy to go . . . OH NO!

That was when I called my boss Tami Thayne and asked her if she had room in her home for a medium sized dog who gets along with other dogs, kids, and cats, and Tami said "Sure, send her over."

Luckily for me, it all happened at a pretty convenient time because Dawn Ashby was passing through Indiana on her way to Pennsylvania for the DDB Valentine stuffing parties, and she detoured to pick up Amy and take her right to Tami.

Now, I was positive that I told Tami that Amy was part monkey but I guess she didn't recall that. *Oops!* Tami being the traveler that she is in her work to spread the word nationwide about chaining, had a big problem on her hands. Her foster dogs had to be pretty safely-contained in her two-fenced-area and doggie-door system, since there were days that employees were only there a couple hours at a time to take care of the fosters. How could she travel the country and keep a monkey disguised as a dog safely contained?

Tami told me about two times that Amy showed her monkey side while in her foster care. She thought she'd outsmarted Amy by containing her inside the office with an indoor fencing unit between her and the doggie door. But no, Amy proceeded to climb the indoor fence, go out through the doggie door, climb the outdoor fence, run through the yard to the other fence, climb over and into that fenced area, and let herself in the top doggie door.

When Tami got home Amy was in a totally different location than where she left her!

On another occasion, all the dogs were safely contained behind the fence, when the UPS guy arrived with a package. They all played their usual game of "Bark at the UPS Guy," which he's well-used to, but he got quite the shock when one of the dogs broke out of the pack, climbed the 6-foot fence, and ran out to meet him! Luckily Tami was right there and able to assure him she was friendly and completely harmless.

Somehow, though, being the cute little button dog that Amy was, she drew the perfect home to within a few short weeks after Tami placed her on Petfinder.

She now lives as part of a family in Pittsburgh, with a sister dog, three kids, and a work-at-home mom. She walks on a leash, and she's only out in the yard when someone's watching. Even then, the 'easy' fence to climb is between her and their good friends yard, so if she does climb the fence, she will be safely contained in the neighbor's yard.

We think.

The Chained
Rescues' Rescue

BY DAWN ASHBY, DDB ILLINOIS REP

℘

Dawn goofing off with her canine companions

Before you start reading let me warn you this is not a rescue story about the rescue of chained dogs. It is, instead, a story about some rescued chained dogs' rescue. Or so I believe. It was their intention and attempt at rescue. Other opinions may vary, but I like to think I've been a good influence on my dogs.

My evening was spent shopping with my eldest daughter. Upon our return home, as we pulled into the driveway, we saw a pack of dogs running toward our house, the biggest with something in his mouth we couldn't make out. They all disappeared into the front door. Simultaneously, we saw my husband and father of my children run out the back door, in his bare feet, and duck behind my car.

He was screaming, "They're your !@#$ dogs, you deal with it!"

Now the fact that the dogs were running loose didn't surprise me. For some reason I can spend every day with these dogs without a problem, but as soon as my husband is in charge they have a way of getting the better of him and escaping.

I knew where they'd been as I saw where they were coming from; there's a city dump for lawn clippings, dead trees, and such down a small road near my house. This area is full of little critters and various and sundry other unsavory objects, and the dogs love to go there to see what they can dig up.

I calmly asked my husband what he was referring to when he said for me to "deal with it." He, not as calmly, replied, "They brought a 'possum into the house!"

On these rare escapes the dogs have brought into our home the legs of slaughtered deer, a dead frog, a decomposing rat and a smelly old fish, so of course I was expecting to find the opossum in such a lifeless state.

Instead, inside the house, when I rounded the corner from the kitchen into the dining room, yes my lovely dining room used for traditional holiday and birthday parties, I found a live opossum hissing at me and rearing its front paw. I immediately called for backup from my trusted canines, all five of which had passed out on the living room floor.

"Come on! Get it! Get it!" I commanded. Only one of those previously chained dogs raised his head before plopping it back down on the carpet.

I turned to Romeo, my Saint Bernard, for help, he who had brought the critter in without harming it in the first place. I was confident he could return it to the outside in the same unscathed manner.

I knew this from experience. One time a rabbit had built a nest in our fenced backyard. I blame the rabbit for this misfortune because what kind of dumb bunny builds a nest and has babies in a back yard filled with numerous and maniacal canines? I ask you?

Well, of course the dogs found the baby bunnies and luckily I was able to round up the dogs and drag them inside, all except for Romeo who was very curious and picked up one of the babies in his mouth. In order to rescue the rabbit from his big stinky breath jowl I climbed onto Romeo's back and proceeded to shake his head fervently by holding on to the back of his collar.

To any passerby it would have looked as if I was trying to ride a Saint Bernard bronco style. But for me, I was merely trying to shake the bunny from his mouth.

"Drop!" Shake shake. "The!" Shake shake. "Bunny!" Shake shake. "Drop!" Shake shake. "The!" Shake shake "Bunny!" Romeo would then drop the bunny and as the rabbit plopped from his mouth onto the grass and proceeded to hop away, he'd see it again, say to himself, "Look a rabbit!" and chase and scoop it up in his jaws all over again.

I finally took hold of the situation and threw myself down on the dog, holding him in place, while the bunny made a clean getaway. After this episode I knew two things: It was true that Romeo wasn't the brightest dog in the pack, and it was possible for Romeo to hold an animal in his mouth without hurting it.

I pushed and pulled against his 200-pounds of dead weight, but he lay exhausted on the floor from his recent escapades. He wasn't budging. What to do?

The situation was worsening as my youngest daughter heard the commotion and was now in the dining room trying to feed crackers to the opossum and asking if we could keep it. It was already after 11:00 p.m., but deeming this an emergency, I dialed the animal control officer at his home and asked for his help.

He was in bed asleep. I had woken him with my problem. He told me to get a net and catch the opossum and deposit it outside. "Will it bite?" I asked.

Half asleep, he groggily replied, "No, it won't bite. Just get it and take it outside." I didn't believe one sleepy, slurred word of what he told me, but in desperation set off to the garage in search of a fishing net. I passed my husband still kneeling behind the car and rolled my eyes. In the garage I found what I was looking for and pulled out the only fishing net we had. It was a goldfish net to catch the Koi in our decorative pond. I pondered the size of the net with my recollection of the mass of the opossum; it wouldn't work.

On my way back inside I noticed my neighbor's kitchen light was on. My neighbor hunted and though I'd never before thought I'd have any use for a hunter living next door, I put two and two together and thought that hunters probably fished as well.

I knocked on his door and asked if he had a proper fishing net as I described to him my dilemma. He went to his garage and came back with a net big enough to "Free Willy" and then he offered to help wrangle up the critter.

In one fell swoop my neighbor secured the opossum—now playing dead—in the net and carried it out the door to be released in a nearby field.

He came back with the triumphant news of his success just as my husband strutted back inside, saying, "I woulda' handled it myself, but I didn't have my shoes on."

I responded to my husband, as well as everyone else within earshot, "Not having shoes on didn't stop you from running out the back door, down the driveway, and hiding behind my car!"

Our neighbor couldn't quell his chuckle, and I hoped the story he could tell made it worth coming out in the middle of the night.

As for the dogs, well, they were a bit dumbfounded. They rescued this creature who looked dead but wasn't, brought it home to mommy as a gift, and after all their trouble I just threw their gift back outside without a word of thanks.

I'm pretty sure they thought since they were rescued and brought into my home, they were "Paying It Forward," of sorts, to the opossum.

Their intentions were pure. Or at least that's how I like to think of it.

Frankie
Ol' Blue Eyes, Georgia Cover Boy

BY PAM CHEATHAM, DDB GEORGIA REP

❧

My email address is on several distribution lists which means I receive 400 emails per day asking for *Last Chance, Urgent* help for dogs in Georgia, the Southeast and sometimes all over the world. Some of these dogs are victims of neglect or they're abandoned. Some have already been taken to the local shelter, where the dog might have a limited number of days to be rescued or adopted before he's on death row. We're stuck with this status quo system until citizens and our government wake up enough to realize that spending tax dollars killing orphaned dogs is not acceptable. It costs less to work with volunteer networks and adopt out the dogs.

Harley (now known as Frankie) was on this day another picture in my inbox, this one in Coweta County, Georgia. The description written by the shelter worker described Harley as having gorgeous blue eyes. That he did.

I couldn't tell much about Harley from the picture. But I knew he'd spent the first 4 years of his life chained in the back of the yard. His owners took him to the shelter to "be put down." He was thin and lethargic and the shelter workers figured he was probably full of parasites and wouldn't live that much longer anyway.

For three days I kept looking at the picture of that blue-eyed dog. Besides our three dogs, we also had two foster dogs who were housed in separate areas of the home while I readied them for adoption. I told myself I didn't have room, but I couldn't believe a rescue group had not yet come forward for this beautiful boy. The clock was winding down.

Lisa Compton, our Virginia DDB rep, was arranging to have some black dogs pulled from the Coweta shelter and sent to rescue when Jeanne Prine, her fellow rescuer in GA, asked "What about Ol' Blue Eyes?"

His time was up and the shelter workers thought he was a kind soul; they hoped a rescuer would notice him and save his life. Lisa lives hundreds of miles from Georgia; maybe that distance or some special nudge from above made it easier for Lisa to say "Okay, pull him." Because that's just what she did.

The next morning, trying to cover herself, she emailed all six Georgia DDB reps, asking if any of us could foster Harley. When I read Lisa's plea, I started to cry. This blue-eyed dog I'd watched for days was sentenced to death— but Lisa had gotten him his reprieve. By God, if Lisa could do that, then I could step up and do my part for him.

I knew I couldn't exactly take him home. But I could take him to my vet.

Next came Ellen. Ellen is one of those rare and oh-so-appreciated rescuers who, when asked, will go pick up/pull a dog, take him to her vet, get him ready for the next step and then deliver him to the rescuer. In this case, Ellen and I agreed to meet at a hotel parking lot on Virginia Avenue where she would hand Ol' Blue Eyes over to me. We quit calling him Ol' Blue Eyes and settled on Frankie, figuring he needed a new name to go with his fresh start.

As I drove up to Ellen's parked car, I could see Frankie sitting next to her in the front seat. He looked so small. *Whoa, that's a German Shepherd?* He looked more like a long-legged Beagle with strange ears. He was skinny and skittish and his hair was thin and falling out, but I could tell he'd already started to bond with Ellen.

Frankie had been through a lot in the past week, but he seemed to be enjoying the attention. At my vet in Conyers we discovered that Frankie would need heartworm treatment in addition to all the other medical care which he'd never received.

While he stayed at the vet, I arranged to pick him up periodically to take him to our property for training and playtime.

Soon we moved him into our house, where we'd leash walk for about four miles a day, then we'd open the gates to the pasture. As I unhooked the leash, he would take off like a shot into the field. Imagine being chained 24/7 for years, then suddenly having the ability to run and play with complete abandon! Freedom was so good for Frankie . . .

Though I had taught Frankie most of the commands, I believe in a structured, positive, group obedience class, especially for Shepherds. So we joined Frogs 2 Dogs training class in East Atlanta.

Frankie was doing well and coming into his own, so when I got my first promising adoption applicant, I was nervous but hopeful. Jordan and Cheryl had cared for a GSD who looked like Frankie so when they saw his picture they wanted to adopt him, provided he got along with Weasel, their kitten.

Oh boy. It wasn't that he didn't like Weasel—he liked him too much. After nearly a month, Cheryl tearfully said goodbye to Frankie before there was an early demise for Weasel.

During Frankie's time with us, we were usually in some kind of training. Besides Frogs 2 Dogs, Frankie attended Angie Woods' US Canine Dog Pack Behavior boot camp where he took even one step further to become a stellar animal companion.

I was so proud and remember so clearly the day Frankie received his diploma from Frogs 2 Dogs. As we walked back to the car along several blocks of leaf-strewn sidewalks on a fresh Fall Sunday afternoon, I began to cry.

I looked down at my blue-eyed boy and told him how pleased I was. He didn't start life very well, wasn't given advantages like some dogs. He could have given up, gotten lazy, gained weight, climbed fences and gotten in with a bad pack. Not Frankie.

He had his diploma and was ready to find his place in the world.

As fate would have it, the very next day a woman named Jan called. She'd seen Frankie's flyer and her family was very interested in meeting him. But she said they had a cat named Pearl. Uh-oh.

When I drove Frankie to meet Jan and her family, there was a hint of crisp early fall chill in the air. It was dark by the time we arrived at the beautiful, large home on a lovely street. Within an hour all the children from the neighboring homes had come out to meet Frankie, and he loved it!

At first Jan, Tom and the kids had to carefully manage Frankie's access to Pearl, their cat. Their patience and diligence paid off.

Jan reports that once the dog door was installed, Frankie was much more independent. He still runs with Jan on leash each morning, but

now he uses the door to go out and chase squirrels. Jan said, "As you know, Pearl and Frankie have become very companionable—although they don't really "hang out" together, they greet each other at the door, nose to nose, when one comes in from outside."

Frankie, with Collette and Jack

We don't know much about Frankie's life when he was chained. Maybe there wasn't much about that time worth remembering. He sure has made up for it with his new life and his new family.

Jack, who was seven at the time, wrote a paper about his new dog and how much he meant to the family. Frankie's habit each night is to nap in Jack's bed and then at 10:00 p.m. switch rooms to sleep in his own bed in Jan and Tom's room.

I knew Frankie deserved better, but I think he's won the lottery! From a chain, to a cell, then on to a mansion on a hill.

Makes me proud to be a Dogs Deserve Better rep.

"I Object, Your Honor"

BY TAMIRA CI THAYNE, DDB FOUNDER

℘

Doogie, after rescue, standing and walking

I'm in a courtroom, again. I sometimes wonder if the pain of court will ever go away. Seems that in order to fight for justice for animals (or any socially disadvantaged group) you must endure repeated assassinations on your character, your motivations, your morals, and your "inability to obey the law."

This day we're in court for the second time attempting to take the owners (I've really been trying not to use this word, but damn if these people don't just see the dogs as property!) of Doogie for abuse charges. But to even take them for abuse, we must go over the DA's head, for he's been blocking us, calling the charges unmerited and a waste of his office's time.

43

Oh, and against his policy, since according to him I took the dog only for my own ego and for financial gain.

If you don't know "the Doogie story," or have forgotten since it began a good three years previous to this, Doogie was a Shepherd-mix dog who lived chained for life. Nothing unusual about that, since these are precisely the dogs we work on behalf of, but in Doogie's case he'd gotten to his elder years and needed medical assistance, like all old dogs do.

His caretakers, or those who were supposed to be caring for him, merely left him there, chained, suffering, unable to stand, and flailing about in the mud and his own feces. They did not take him to the vet, but instead went about their business, riding ATVs, cutting their grass, etc.

Meanwhile, the dog lay on the wet ground, crying for help, his pleas ignored. The neighbor across the street sent her husband over, asking the caretakers to give the dog aid. The man of the house al-legedly walked out, propped Doogie up, and walked back into the house.

Doogie promptly fell back over again.

The neighbor, Kim, cried all weekend as she watched him suf-fer. She called 911 (although this call has mysteriously disappeared), where she was told to call the Humane Society. It was Saturday, and the Central Pennsylvania Humane Society doesn't work weekends; she left a message and kept vigil, waiting, all through the long days of Saturday and Sunday.

Monday morning came and still she received no call back.

Now she was frantic. Having watched the dog deteriorate all weekend, she didn't know how much longer he could hold on with-out the help he so desperately needed.

She called Dogs Deserve Better around 10:00 a.m. Monday morn-ing, and my assistant spoke to her. I was informed that there was a chained dog unable to stand or walk in East Freedom—on the other side of the county—and was asked what we should do. I told her to have Kim call the Humane Society again, leaving a *very* detailed message about the urgency of the situation, and hopefully they would respond immediately.

Around noon we got a call from another woman who works with Kim confirming the condition of the dog, and telling us she'd seen him on the ground that morning too. I knew if we didn't take action, we would be just as morally wrong as the dog's caretakers; for knowing about abuse and doing nothing is virtually the same as doing it yourself.

I called Kim back and told her we'd come out to see the dog and make a plan from there. Oftentimes people exaggerate the condition of the dog, and I hoped that this was one of those times. It was now past noon, and she still had not received a return call from the Humane Society.

Upon arrival at Doogie's residence, I saw him from the road, lying prone, completely still, back to us, and I told my assistant, "We're too late, he's already dead."

But when we got out and went over to him, he raised his head and looked at us pleadingly, as if to say, "I beg of you, please don't walk away." No one was home, so I videotaped his inability to stand, and instructed my assistant to photo document the case while Kim and I worked to get him into the van for an emergency trip to the vet.

The humane officer met us at the vet (he knows where we take our rescues), CARRIED the dog into the vet's office for us, told me he was going to get a warrant, and to call him later on his super-secret-police-cell-phone-that-he-always-answers-except-as-it-turns-out-when-I-call-him-about-Doogie.

The vet x-rayed Doogie and found that he had, at a minimum, bone spurs in his back which caused him too much pain to walk or stand, plus he was dehydrated and malnourished, with sores and bare areas on his legs and torso. He gave Doogie a shot of painkiller mixed with vitamins and sent him home with me, insisting that he "deserved a chance to pull through and to know life."

When safely ensconced at my home and after giving Doogie the much-needed water, food, and a bath, I called the humane officer on his super-secret-police-cell-phone-that-he-always-answers-except-as-it-turns-out-when-I-call-him-about-Doogie. He didn't answer, and I left a message telling him I had Doogie at my home, asking if he had obtained the warrant, and how he wanted me to proceed from here.

He never called back.

Around 5:00 p.m. I got a call from the East Freedom police asking if I had the dog. I told the officer that I did indeed have the dog, but I had photos and video evidence of abuse, would he like to see them? He said no, he wasn't interested in my evidence, and that I had two choices: to return the dog to the abusers or be arrested myself.

This was the quintessential make-or-break moment in my life: I must now choose whether to be coward or queen.

I didn't want to be arrested. I didn't want to be humiliated, I didn't want to go to court, and I didn't want to be a criminal. I wanted to be a good little girl.

But more than I didn't want all those bad things for myself, I didn't want the dog back in a situation that was criminal and downright deadly for him—whether the police recognized his rights or not.

I had to put the dog's needs first.

I pronounced he'd have to arrest me.

I got the dog out of my home, uploaded the video to YouTube, created an e-mail about the situation, and waited. It was around 9:00 p.m. when three squad cars and the people who to my mind are the

REAL criminals appeared in my driveway. I pushed send on the e-mail to our supporters and walked out to meet my fate.

I was handcuffed, put in the back of a dark squad car, and driven 30 miles to the East Freedom police station, where I was arrested, later arraigned, and dumped out onto the streets of Hollidaysburg at 2:00 a.m.—no ride home and no money.

The Police Chief, a lover of power plays, told the arresting officer within earshot that "if I ever touched his dog he'd put a cap in my ass." He treated me like a piece of dirt until the moment the magistrate was assessing my flight risk and I told her I had served in the Air Force. Being an ex-Marine himself, his head shot up and he looked at me with new-found respect. I still had none for him.

He advised the magistrate to charge me $50,000 bond for this lowest level misdemeanor, since I was apparently a hardened criminal despite having no previous arrests. She didn't go for that, telling him she saw no reason for it, and charged $10,000 unsecured bond, which meant that I was free to leave without paying any money.

The jury trial that ensued over a year later was a mockery of true justice. The judge and DA virtually instructed the jury to find me guilty without exception, which they obliged to do within thirty minutes. There were prospective jurors who were tossed out of the jury pool without ceremony because they said they'd never convict me for my actions.

I wonder how those who did convict me look themselves in the eye each morning. I've seen a few of them around town since the trial and not one of them can meet my gaze.

As a matter of fact, NONE of them can meet my gaze and hold it. Not the DA, the judge, the jurors, the abusers, the cop, or the humane officer. None of them. For me, this fact alone speaks volumes.

I'm still shocked that there wasn't one person on the jury who had a true sense of right and wrong and was willing to stand in the light of that conviction. Sometimes I am so very disappointed in the human race. Mind you, it was Friday afternoon at 5:00 p.m. and I'm sure they all wanted to get home to their dinners, their families, and their after-trial drinks, all so much more important than doing the right thing and sending a message to abusers that animals are worthy of protection too.

When they came out to deliver the verdict I knew it would be "guilty" because it was too quick for an innocent. I didn't want to give them the satisfaction of seeing me cry, so I looked down at my notebook and frantically scribbled "I'm a big brave dog" over and over again to distract myself from the pain of the betrayal. My son Rayne used to say that all the time when he was little and afraid to do something, and I'd always thought it was cute. I needed to both give myself courage and to feel that connection to a human who loved and respected me during a very sad and painful moment of my life.

I was later sentenced to 300 hours community service for a people nonprofit, for which I was supposed to pay a fee of $5.00 per hour, ($1500 total), as well as pay for juror's lunches, extra sheriff time, my probation officer, and various and sundry other everyday court fees.

Mind you, once again, that this crime was the lowest-level misdemeanor, theft of a piece of property valued at $0-$50. In essence, me stealing Doogie was little more than stealing a pack of gum! Yet I was sentenced to much more than would be normal for this crime level, in an obvious attempt by the judge to "teach me a lesson."

I've always wondered what the lesson was that she was so diligently trying to teach me. Let dogs die if they are in other people's yards? Don't fight back when you are wrongly accuse and arrested? Don't stand up to those who abuse you or someone else? Don't stand in your own God-given power?

What? What was the lesson there, judge?

Flash-forward to three years later, and we are still fighting for charges to go the other way; for the so-called guardians of Doogie to be charged with cruelty for their failure to provide him with veterinary care, as required by Pennsylvania law.

Funny thing is, it's a summary offense only, so even IF we were to get a conviction, they would get much less punishment than I did for helping the dog. Go figure.

But we have to get there first. We first filed a private criminal complaint about eight months after the incident when it became obvious that the police and the humane officer were not doing their jobs. The magistrate sent back the paperwork to be refiled against both the husband and wife separately, then recused himself from the case because he was the same magistrate that I had gone before.

The case then fell into limbo. Every time my attorney asked the DA what was going on with it, he received no response at all.

Finally, we filed papers to force him to address the case. He denied the case, based solely on "what a bad person Tammy Grimes (my former name) is." It cites things such as:

1. I did it all for publicity. (What, forced the guardians to leave their dog lay flailing on the ground so I could sweep in and be arrested? Force everyone in the so-called law enforcement chain of command to ignore the condition of the dog? *Who could even know that all these people would be so corrupt?*)

2. I wanted to be a hero. (Again, see above.)

3. I did it for financial gain. (And yet again, see above.)

4. He has a policy against "vigilantes." This is one of his kinder labels for me, and seems almost like a compliment. Hey, Batman was labeled a vigilante too, so maybe I could buy a cape and make my unofficial title more legitimate.

I'm embarrassed to admit to you, after all this, that I did everything I could to get OUT of going over there that day, because I didn't want to end up in the place where I had to make the decision I ended up having to make. I wanted to be the cowardly little girl who stayed home and buried her head under the covers and pretended nothing bad was happening. But Fate forced me to stand up for the dog; he certainly couldn't do it for himself.

Finally, we get before the judge in our attempt to go over the DA's head, and it turns out to be the same judge who sentenced me in my arrest case. She too is convinced I'm the spawn of Satan (see left to review the specific points of my Sataninity), so my attorney asks her to recuse herself. She does.

That leads us to now, three months past that point and a good three years after the initial sighting of Doogie, attempting to once again force the DA to allow the private criminal complaint to go through.

I happen to be feeling pretty good about my life right now.

Not so in the year following the trial, by far the worst of my life. Not only did the DA and the judge say (and the papers print) horrible things about me, but I had breeders and your normal everyday chainers floating about the internet trashing me every chance they got.

Some folks like you DID think I was a hero—which is not a bad thing as the judge and DA would lead you to believe—but being a woman, I tended to ignore the good things people said and take all the bad to heart, letting it rip me apart.

Not only was I trying to hold my head above water with the Doogie trial, but my ex—lovely fellow that he is—decided now would be a good time to bust a move and finally take possession of our daughter the way he'd always wanted to do. After all, how could I possibly fight two court battles at once; he was sure to win!

He did win. I fell apart, decided I would never step foot in a courtroom (which I equated to the depths of Hell) again, and refused to go. He gladly took her off my hands, his possession, and I laid in bed weeping for three months. It was all I could do to keep from throwing the organization away, throwing my life away. I wanted to die. I blubbered, I whined, I pitied myself, then I got up and did whatever DDB work I had to do to get by before crawling back into bed and starting the whole process over again.

Eventually I began to pick myself off the floor, and started to fight for my life and my self-esteem. I sought help—not with a counselor, but with a best-friend healing trip to Sedona, Arizona, and through books I felt led to purchase and read.

Above all else, I began cultivating a positive attitude, and putting into practice what I'd learned in my favorite book, *Excuse Me, Your Life is Waiting*, by Lynn Grabhorn. When I felt down, I worked very hard not to stay in that emotional place, forcing myself to think and most importantly FEEL positive emotions in order to bring myself back up.

Little by little things changed. I spent the next year as my own lawyer fighting for my daughter in court. I got over some of my intimidation of the system, and learned how abusive this system is toward women. I had a couple small victories, but when I finally got back before a judge again—as is often the case in parental alienation custody cases—he disbelieved everything I said, sided with my ex, and continued to give him most of the time with our daughter.

I wish I could say that I'm at peace with my daughter's situation, but I'm not, and I never will be. You cannot take a child from her mother, a child who this mother bore without a single painkiller, a child who I breastfed for 2-1/2 years, and expect that I will just say "Fine" and walk away. Will never happen.

I accept that it is what it is, that there is no way I will win in court and that a system which favors abusive males now has control of my child. I have made the decision to move on with my life and find happiness elsewhere as I can. My daughter will always be welcome to live with me if she chooses, and I pray that someday I will get a chance to form a better relationship with her.

I have a partner now who I love and cherish more than anything in the world. This man lights up my life in a way that no other man ever has or ever will. He loves me exclusively, and he shows me his love on a daily, even an hourly, basis.

He has taught me that not all men will hurt me, not all men are abusers, and not all men are like the DA, my father, and my ex-husband. Some men are truly good men, truly men who value women, and truly men who we can in turn value.

I've written *Scream Like Banshee: 29 Days of Tips and Tales to Keep Your Sanity as a Doggie Foster Parent*, which has won rave reviews from all three people who read it (yeah, go ahead and laugh). The book has helped not only others through the stress of fostering dogs, but has even saved a dog's life!

I've survived, and I've evolved.

Today, as I sit in court and listen once again to the DA spout lies about me that no good woman should have to hear, I've grown strong enough to seriously contemplate jumping from my seat and yelling:

"I OBJECT, YOUR HONOR!"

I Object, Your Honor, to having to listen to the DA's lies about me, twisted lies that only a twisted man could tell.

I Object, Your Honor, to feeling like I am once again on trial when this case is not about me, but solely about abuse of a dog, abuse of a dog that belonged—a mere piece of property—to another who was morally and legally obligated for his welfare.

I Object, Your Honor, to the court's patriarchical rulings, to the way it intimidates those who've been victims of abuse into keeping their mouths shut, and deeming them wrong even in the absolute telling of truth.

For, despite what you think, DA, and despite what any judge in any courtroom in America says, I know that I was morally and ethically right for helping a dog who went from flailing on the ground to knowing six months of joy, freedom, chain-free living, and human love.

I know that Doogie's 'owners' were not only morally and ethically wrong in their failure to meet his needs, but legally wrong too. I know this to the depths of my being.

Even if I do not win today in your court of law, I know that I have already won in the court of God's laws. It won't always be enough, but for today, it just may have to be.

Basement Beasts:
The Story of Annie and Belle

BY DAN AND CINDY MCGILL, DDB OHIO REPS

⅋

Annie, severely underweight, just after rescue from the basement

My wife Cindy and I had just begun looking again into the world of dog rescue at the beginning of summer. This is something Cindy has always been interested in, but her pursuit of any group involvement got put on hold when I deployed to Iraq. I had been medically retired almost a year ago, and the timing was right. We'd watched the videos, cried while reading the stories of abused and neglected dogs, and were eager for the chance to help out a suffering dog. Cindy knew which group she wanted to contact, so she sent Marla Dakes, a Dogs Deserve Better Ohio rep, an email and we met her at a pet fair in Akron.

Cindy and I knew this was the group we wanted to be part of, and now it was time to make it happen. She convinced me that together we could make a difference in a chained/neglected dog's life. We are a team, she and I…

In the beginning of July, not very long after becoming local representatives ourselves, we received an email about two dogs who had been living the past three years confined in a basement in Kent, Ohio. The contact person attached photos which just broke our hearts.

These two beautiful dogs, a six-year-old Bullmastiff and a three-year-old Bordeaux Mastiff, were living in absolute squalor and were very badly malnourished. They were among piles of old feces, trash, and other household refuse. It was as though the basement was their dumping ground for all the unwanted items in the home…including two gorgeous dogs.

We had to do something, and quick. The lady told us the dogs were living in her parents' neighbor's basement. The caretakers were very willing to surrender the dogs, as long as they weren't any part of it—they didn't want to have cruelty charges filed against them.

So they signed over ownership of the dogs to the neighbors. We decided it was in the best interest of the dogs to just get them out of their situation as fast as possible and not bother confronting the people who we knew were abusers and deserved to be prosecuted.

Cindy tried making contact with several pure breed rescues only to be told they wouldn't help us because we weren't sure the dogs were pure breeds. After a few days of hearing "no," we made the choice to bring the dogs into our home, and figure it out from there. The pictures of these dogs were burnt into our minds.

Cindy and I stayed up a few nights in a row worrying about these two poor dogs, and wondering how someone could have let them live like that. We thought up new names for the dogs as we gathered water, dog treats and leashes. We decided the names Annie and Belle would work just fine.

The photos didn't really prepare us for the terrible condition these two beautiful girls were in. Belle, the Bullmastiff, was about 30 pounds underweight, and Annie, the Bordeaux, was about 50 pounds underweight...so skinny and weak she couldn't stand up on her own. She crawled around on her belly.

We gave them a little bit of food, exchanged some words with the people dropping them off and asked them to pass along our disgust to the dogs' owners. One thing they said we will never forget—"The dogs were really loved"—and Cindy said she hoped she never knew that kind of love.

The smell in the car was unbearable. All windows were partly down and the circulating air was of little help. We were thankful we skipped breakfast that morning. Annie and Belle were filthy, they had feces matted into their hair, rotting teeth, and missing fur. Annie had scratches all along her muzzle, evidence of having fought with the bigger Belle over what little scraps of food they could find. They had no social skills whatsoever, and didn't seem to realize what was happening to them at first.

Straight to the veterinarian's office we went. Belle barked at everyone and every thing on the way in and poor Annie had to be carried in. We got their shots and checkups over with and took them home for a nice, long bath.

I don't think I've ever seen bathwater this filthy; but after a lot of squirming and splashing, the ladies were cleaned up and ready to explore their new house. They met our forever dogs, Jake and Lucas, and the rest of the family, and all of a sudden it seemed they understood they were safe and with people who cared about them. They relaxed and even went to sleep on our couch, snoring loudly and cuddled together.

It would be several weeks of long, hard work to get any weight on the girls and get them housebroken.

Annie was finally able to walk and run around outside, and Belle was wagging her tail so much it began to bleed from being whacked against corners in the house.

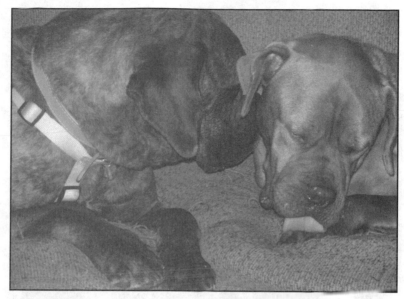

They were so happy to be out of that basement dungeon they'd suffered in for years. It turned out that Annie and Belle had been locked in the basement of that house for at least three years without being allowed outside for anything other than a few minutes sometimes. With little if any human contact and little food, they fended for themselves.

I don't care to imagine what they found to eat, and how they survived down there; I'm just glad they did.

Watching these two, it occurred to us that they had no idea how to be dogs. They didn't know what to do with toys, had never been leash trained, and didn't seem to know what it meant to have a belly rub or a scratch behind the ears. Being locked in that basement was merely an exercise in survival, trying to make it through even one more day. What a terrible, lonely existence for a dog.

When it became apparent that Annie wouldn't be able to move forward in her re-adjustment without being removed from the more dominant Belle, we put Belle in a foster home. The new foster home fell in love with this massive beast, and she lives there still. She's continuing to make great improvements—gaining back most of her weight, calming down a bit on the tail wagging, with a great family that loves and cares for her. She's the queen of her new castle!

Annie required a little more hard labor…she didn't like any of the men in the house at first, but clung to Cindy very closely. She became Cindy's shadow.

Annie went through a heat cycle, and we learned that big dogs need diapers…who knew? She didn't like wearing them any more than we liked putting them on her, and we're hoping to catch any future rescue girls and get them spayed BEFORE the heat cycle hits!

It took nearly a month to get Annie to socialize with our two dogs, but when she did, it was a wonderful sight to behold. Annie was evolving into an amazing dog right before our eyes.

Annie learned how to walk on a leash but not before the wild flowers in our front yard were rolled over and stomped. We didn't mind much…the little girl was still getting accustomed to being outside.

Cindy worked very hard with Annie on leashing and housebreaking, and when the time came to put Annie up for adoption to a new home, we knew it had to be the PERFECT one.

Several applications came through, but none of them were a match for Annie's special needs. One finally did, and it seemed like divine intervention that these people who so loved their family pets that they'd rebuilt their entire back yard and porch to accommodate them were interested in Annie.

Cindy wept and held Annie in her arms the day we went to drop her off at her new home. We knew it was for the best, but we couldn't help but feel a little sad that we had to let go of this beautiful creature.

Annie now lives in a beautiful home in Columbia Station, Ohio, with another dog almost as docile and sweet as she is, Zeus, and two absolutely amazing parents.

They keep us updated on her progress, and she too is now on the fast-track to full recovery. She's claimed a large armchair in her new home, where she perches, keeping a close eye on things that go on with her new family. We have no doubt that for the rest of Annie's life she'll never want for food or love again, and she has probably already forgotten the horrors of being locked in a filthy, damp basement, and nearly starved to death.

Annie and Belle have forever changed our lives; it brings such huge smiles to our faces to see their updated pictures and stories.

Because of Annie's submissive nature, I think she desperately needed Cindy's mothering abilities. The two of them created a bond that I am not sure I understand but I do know Annie took a big piece of Cindy's heart with her, and I think Annie left a piece of hers with Cindy. The two will be entwined forever.

Dancing
with Layla

BY BELEN BRISCO, DDB FLORIDA REP

ဇ

Layla, stuck under the fence, begging for help

I'd like to share a story about a big beautiful blonde, our rescue dog Layla. She weighs in now at approximately 80 pounds and has the most incredible soft brown eyes. Her paws reach up to my husband's shoulders, which is quite amazing since my husband is 6'4". She wraps her arms around his shoulders and looks as though she is asking him to dance.

My husband understands that Layla is the only big beautiful blonde allowed to do this.

Layla wasn't always as happy and healthy as she is today. Born in Texas she was a gift for a young man who moved to Florida. I happened to meet that young man in April after receiving a call from a good friend of mine who noticed that Layla was not only on a short chain, but hadn't been able to reach food or water in days. You see this gift became too much trouble to keep in the house so she was tethered out back and forgotten.

The tether became entangled and there she sat—in the heat, the rain, and the dampness of night. She could peer through a hole in the fence and any passerby with a heart could not help but to look upon her with sadness.

One night I received the call from my friend Drew.

"Belen, there is a dog in my neighborhood and I think she might be dead or dying." Not the thing you want to hear. "Can you help?"

"Of course I can or I will do my best." I said.

By the time, I finished my conversation with him; I began making calls immediately to the animal control officers and to 911 to get the police involved. I also called my good friend and representative of Dogs Deserve Better in Arlington, Texas, Nili. Thank goodness she was awake. I consider it rude to call anyone after 9:00 p.m. but this was a dog emergency.

I told her the story and that the dog was about 45 minutes away; that my family was asleep, but I was still considering going out alone to see if I can help this dog. She talked me into not going alone at that night, but to wait until morning. Good call. My husband would have been worried had he awakened and found me missing, I'm sure! So, I called my friend Drew back and asked if he would monitor her through the night, as he was so close by.

"Drew can you get her water and food through the hole in the fence and watch her through the night?"

He said, "You mean like a covert operation?"

"Yes, Drew, that is what I mean." I replied.

Now that the situation had become top secret, our mission to help this hostage intrigued Drew. The night was long and my first call of the morning was to Drew.

"Yes, she's fine. She's still alive." He reported, like a good soldier.

Animal control was out first thing as well and had made it one of their top priorities, but since the guardian was not there, only a warning could be issued. They were kind enough to speak to me through my friend Drew's phone and tell me the situation. They did their job, lacking as we sometimes feel it is, and now it was my turn.

With food, water, leash and camera in hand (never leave home without those) I was off. My husband saw to it that my SUV had all the essentials as well. My husband and I called off the items, Ladder? *Check!* (Just in case I had to climb the fence—with permission of course.)

Towel? *Check!* (Just in case the pup needed to be dried off from sitting in the elements.) Most of all, Cell phone? *Check!* (Just in case I got in over my head and had to call him.) OK, I was set.

I arrived at the scene and there she was, peering through the hole in the fence like a forlorn and forgotten child. I proceeded to give her water—she wouldn't take it; food—not while I was still sitting in the god-forsaken mud hole.

So I gave her the most important thing, pats on the head—OK, she will accept those.

Then I noticed tags around her neck with a phone number. *Do I dare try to call the phone number? Why not?* I thought as I dialed the number on the tag on my cell phone.

Can you believe I actually reached the caretaker? To my amazement he was also originally from Texas, like me, so we had that in common. Good way to begin a friendly conversation.

Now comes the hard part. "Sir, did you know your dog is in a dire situation?"

His response was, "No. My goodness what happened?"

Ok, he admits he lives here, knows he has a dog so how could he not know that this poor girl on a chain waits for him to come home and relieve her of her loneliness and hunger? We spoke some more about his dog's needs. After a few moments, he admitted he didn't want to keep her any longer.

"Your lucky day," I said, "I can take her."

So, with his permission, we untangled Layla, got her on a leash and all the surrounding neighbors came outside to cheer us on and shout for joy! They too had been watching this poor girl suffer and didn't know what to do about it.

By early afternoon, Layla was in the vet's office, courtesy of Dogs Deserve Better. She was my first rescue, and Kim at the DDB home office OK'd the vetting and had the vet's office fax her the bill. This is a great system for us reps scattered all about the country, and great for the dogs to get the immediate vet care they need.

Layla was heartworm negative and now up to date on all shots but needed to gain some weight. She is a Great Pyrenees mix, but only weighing in at about 69 pounds and with a bit of a skin condition called "hot spots" on her body. The vet felt that soon she would be just fine.

My friend Drew fostered her for a couple of weeks while we found a forever home for her. Her first adopter didn't take long to realize that Layla wasn't working out for their lifestyle. Layla was suffering from separation anxiety and this new adopter was gone much of the day.

She came back to stay with us in our home with our pack until we can find the perfect adopter for her. She deserved that much, some time to get back to her healthy weight and get back on her feet.

Today she is strong, beautiful, and as kind as any dog can be. She is the guardian of the pack. We have someone coming to meet her and they are excited at the prospect of having Layla be in their forever home.

I have a lot of love for this big girl. They say things are bigger in Texas and she is proof with a heart as big as the Lone Star State itself. Thank you Dogs Deserve Better for giving me the tools to help this beautiful dog.

In the words of country singer, Lee Ann Womack, "Living might mean taking chances, but they're worth taking. Lovin' might be a mistake, but it's worth making. Don't let some hell bent heart leave you bitter. When you come close to selling out, reconsider. Give the heavens above more than just a passing glance. And when you get the choice to sit it out or dance. I hope you dance."

Dance Layla, dance.

A Rescuer's
Promise

BY KATHLEEN SLAGLE, DDB PENNSYLVANIA REP

ℬ

One of the Canadensis dogs before rescue

In February a local rescue group was called to a home in Canadensis, Pennsylvania, to pick up some puppies the caretakers couldn't sell, so now they wanted to 'get rid of' them. They were told if they didn't come right away (a common threat) that the puppies would be left in a box on the side of the road. There had been a news report the previous winter when someone found a box of puppies along a road in the same area, so assuming it was the same abusers, the rescue group wasted no time getting there.

They arrived at the property to find eight dogs chained outside, several of which had given birth to the puppies weeks earlier. Most of the puppies were living outside with the mother dogs and were quite sick. Temperatures were in the teens at night and the makeshift doghouses were completely sub-standard. To complete this nightmare scenario, there was a Husky mix that had been chained to a nearby doghouse, but was now lying dead on a woodpile.

Once the puppies were safely removed I received a call from the rescue to see if Dogs Deserve Better would help with the chained dogs. With the landowner's permission I visited the property in order to assess the situation.

Notice her 'house' and her nipples from repeatedly bearing puppies

I could feel I was being watched from inside the house as I set about documenting the scene—noting the details of each dog, the gender, breed, any health issues I observed. The general area was simply atrocious, just dirt, without a blade of grass anywhere.

One of the doghouses had only a mattress as a roof. Another was nothing more than a pallet on the ground with two pallets leaning against each other to form an inverted "v" shape; added "bonus" was the tarp thrown over the top.

Our local humane officer had been called to the same property months earlier and deemed these shelters as "adequate." How in God's name could she even begin to describe these shelters as "adequate?" No one, and I mean no one with two brain cells to rub together, would *ever* say these houses were adequate for the harsh winter temperatures we experience in this area of Pennsylvania.

The dogs were all thin. One was on a chain that was no more than two feet long—she could barely move and her collar was too tight. Most did not have real collars but pieces of what looked to be leashes cut up and knotted around their necks.

Furthermore, only one of the outside females was spayed. The remaining four females were continuously being impregnated by the inside dog who was allowed to roam free in the yard.

I tried to remain detached from the ghastliness of the situation, until I came to the last dog. He gently jumped up and put his paws on me. There was no more guarding emotions as my heart broke right then and there.

I promised I would get them ALL out one way or another.

I called the guardians a few days later and told them that by utilizing the services of Dogs Deserve Better, I could find all of these dogs inside homes so they wouldn't freeze in the winter. They wouldn't hear of it. I asked if we could get each of the dogs to the vet. They denied needing any assistance other than free dog food.

After several more calls, and once the caretakers learned there would be no cost to them, they reluctantly agreed to allow the dogs to be vetted, but did not want the dogs "fixed."

I am nothing if not persistent.

It took more convincing, but they eventually agreed to allow all of the dogs to be spayed or neutered. Starting that spring, I picked up one or two of the dogs every few weeks and drove them to a vet in nearby New Jersey. The dogs would stay at my house for a day or two before I returned them. This way they had at little time to recover from surgery before going back to the dirt.

You'll never know how difficult it was for me to return each dog. I felt like I was letting them down, and once they had known the love that is possible, the life that was possible, it felt even crueler to take them back to their little patch of dirt. I promised them all, one by one, that I WOULD get them out, one way or another.

The vet found that all of the dogs had hook or roundworms as well as severe flea infestations. Interestingly, the owners denied that any of the dogs had worms, despite me showing them the information from the vet, so I had to sneak the necessary worming medication to the dogs myself.

Several of the dogs were diagnosed with ear infections, and one of the dogs constantly had her head tilted to the side. When I asked one of the guardians when this behavior first started with her, he told me the dog seemed to have gotten "sick" at one point, describing what sounded like a seizure, but said after awhile she seemed ok and they never took her to the vet.

I visited the property several more times over the course of that summer. Only once did I see water in the dogs' bowls. There was one bowl per dog and clearly they were putting food in these bowls. When I questioned one of the guardian's children about the lack of water, they said the dogs were already given water and they must have "drunk it." Whenever I asked if I could give the dogs water from the outside tap, I again met with resistance, and was told "someone would do it later."

Later I found there was no running water in the house, which is why the dogs never had water and why I wasn't allowed to use the tap. They were only giving the dog's small amounts of bottled water mixed in with their food each morning.

Over the course of my visits I would periodically spend time talking to the caregivers. Time and again I looked around at what was once a beautiful home and property, but was now a mess of overgrown weeds, junk cars and eight makeshift dog houses. I asked how they thought this situation was acceptable, to have eight dogs chained in the yard. The woman blurted out all the usual fabrications, such as "we take the dogs for walks all the time," "the dogs saw a vet last year and were ok then," "we take them out in the car for rides all the time," etc.

The man chimed in "Everything's fine. I haven't lost one yet." So I asked about the dead Husky that was on the woodpile when the rescue group first arrived at their property. The woman insisted neighbors who did not like them had poisoned the dog. In a later conversation, the man told me he thought the dog died because he fed him a turkey leg and probably choked.

I could imagine all too vividly what a horrible death that poor dog endured.

Midway through the summer, after much coaxing from me (I told you I was persistent), the guardians agreed to give up four of the dogs. I couldn't let myself truly believe it, as they had agreed to do this several times before, and then changed their minds because they "loved" the dogs so much.

This time I was not going to let the opportunity slip away because of their indecisiveness. I knew I needed to move fast before they changed their minds again. Of course, there was the usual panic of not having anywhere to take the dogs, but with the help of some friends, we found places for each one. The task began of getting to know the dogs and finding suitable homes or fosters.

Since the remaining four dogs left chained on the property were now all vetted, I had no valid reason to continue my visits. I called periodically to see how the dogs were doing, but the voice mail messages I left went unreturned.

I was plagued with many a sleepless night…knowing that there were dogs out there wasting away on the end of those chains, and without committed law enforcement my hands were tied as tightly as those four remaining chained dogs were.

One of the Canadensis dogs after rescue, looking much healthier

One day early in the fall, out of the blue, this same man called me on the phone. He asked me if I could take the remaining dogs for a week or so while they went on vacation. I asked when they were leaving and he said "the day after tomorrow."

Angry they were leaving on vacation in two days and had made no arrangements for the care of the dogs, I told him I didn't run a boarding kennel and the only way I would take the dogs is if he let me keep them and find them homes. After an arduous discussion, he actually agreed!

In the midst of scrambling for places to keep the dogs I visited them, fed them, and gave them water. The guardians were already gone on vacation and in just a few days I was able to get the dogs out of there… forever. The first three dogs were packed into the car, but when I looked around for the last one who had been standing by his doghouse the whole time watching us, he wasn't there. It was eerily quiet and I didn't see him anywhere.

Something brushed against my foot. The grass was high and I assumed it was a snake. Like the brave animal rescuer I am, I was getting ready to scream for dear life! (I rescue the dogs; someone else can look after the snakes, deal?) As I looked down I saw the 80-pound dog playfully lying on his back in the tall grass next to my foot.

Yes, of course, this was the same dog who jumped up on me during my very first visit... my heart melted again. This time, my emotions were running high because I was fulfilling the promise I made earlier in the year, and I couldn't help but finally allow myself to cry a happy tear or two. I was getting every last chained dog out of there. "See pup? I told you I would do it, one way or another!"

But the story doesn't end there. Approximately two weeks later, I received a call from the woman. She told me they returned from their trip and she wanted me to bring the dogs back. I went over the conversation I had with her boyfriend and his subsequent agreement to give the dogs to me. She was furious and insisted that she "loved" these dogs. There was a whole series of calls back and forth over the next week. The boyfriend of course denied there was any agreement to give up the dogs. The woman ended up calling a district magistrate and asking him to press charges. Eventually she backed down when she realized her boyfriend wasn't telling her the truth.

So the long, drawn out saga was finally over and the dogs now all live inside in loving homes. Being able to get these dogs out of that situation, with the help of quite a few dedicated people along the way, was a gift I will never forget.

As a footnote, I recently drove by to check whether the people had started collecting dogs again. The old dilapidated ruins of the doghouses still sit, like empty skeletons reminding me of what was and would still be if I had given up or been too overwhelmed to help the dogs in the first place.

Thankfully today, if you drove by this home, there would be no dogs either seen or heard, unless it was the ghost of the poor husky, the only one unlucky enough not to get out alive.

Two more 'after' photos of the Canadensis dogs.

Radar
Love

BY NILOOFAR ASGHARIAN, DDB TEXAS REP

❧

The puppy whimpered for help, "Please tell me how this device works for I am thirsty and in need of a drink. Please show me how to make the water flow from this pipe, for I can smell it but cannot see it."

Someone did come, but only brought with him a beating to silence the noise of the crying puppy. Then he walked away without even attempting to quench the pup's thirst. Left with the dryness in his throat, the hunger in his belly, the ache of loneliness in his heart, and now the sting of another beating, he wondered why there was so much pain in his existence.

Ironically, Radar was tethered to and tangled about a faucet, yet the puppy rarely had water to drink. For nine months in Fort Worth, Texas, the pup survived with barely any food, water, and without shelter. His guardian beat him often.

Niloofar Asgharian, Nili to her fellow DDB reps, enlisted the help of photographer Char Duncan to document in pictures and record video of the pup's living horror. Through teamwork, Nili incorporated aid from another Dogs Deserve Better representative, Belen Brisco, and several mailings were sent to the Fort Worth Cruelty Investigator encouraging a warrant and seizure.

The Fort Worth Cruelty Investigator delayed moving forward because she felt an established pattern of violations and abuse would win a court case. Though Nili acknowledged the rationale of the procedure, she was overcome with grief and frustrations as she witnessed the little pup continue to suffer only to win favor of the court. It was almost more than Nili could endure.

The wheels of the justice system spin too slowly in the wake of suffering. Often by the time the legal system moves, it is too late for the animal. Judges who maintain that protocol must be followed because they must adhere to the letter of the law do not see or acknowledge the risks to the individual animal by waiting as a case is built and documented.

Rescuers know all to well the torment of waiting and watching, being told not to feed or water a neglected animal for days on end as it will hinder an investigation. We wonder if the abused animal will survive without interference, and more often than not, we give up on the direction of authority if only to lend a small amount of relief with a drink of water or the tossing of a treat.

Nili waited. Finally, just when she was about to give up hope, the Fort Worth Cruelty Investigator obtained a warrant for seizure and won the subsequent court case against the abuser. Nili rescued Radar through Dogs Deserve Better Radar, and gratefully accepted the assistance of Jerry and Shannon Borders who fostered, trained and brought back to her a gentle, sweet pup who was even good with her five rescue cats.

Quietly, Nili cried to Radar, "Tell me little one, have I done right by you? Have I taken away your sorrows and replaced them with joy? Your belly is full, your dish is always replenished with water, you are free to play and wander about my home, to enjoy long walks, toys, treats, snuggles, and are no longer tangled and tethered to misery. Can you forgive humankind for your mistreatment at the beginning of your life, now that all your days until the end will be filled with love? Tell me my small friend, are you happy now?"

A soft kiss to the back of Nili's hand and with a wag of his tail Radar answered, "Yes, I forgive humanity, I am happy with you, and I will remain always faithful to you."

For Radar, who once existed tethered to a water spigot while nearly perishing from thirst, had already curled up on the couch and forgotten all abuse he had suffered at the hands of man. Such is the way of the dog.

Hokie's
Choice

BY SHANNON EATON ALLEN, DDB VIRGINIA REP

ℬ

Shannon snuggles Hokie on the bed

News of spring came late to the mountains. The Appalachian morning was spitting snow, entirely unaware it was the 28th of April. My husband, our six four-legged babies (seven including the cat), and I were moving from a small town to an even smaller one, a mere ten-mile change but thrilling nonetheless. All six of the dogs and the lone feline were worn out from moving and they didn't even carry the boxes.

We'd been zipping back and forth down a winding mountain road that hugged a creek bank as we bounced from our old house to the new for several days. At times we fought farm trucks for a just a sliver of the pavement. During one such trip, we choose an alternate route. We felt we deserved a change of scenery and the fast food luncheon awaiting our arrival at our new town's gas station. We dined lavishly, put off picking up one more box for as long as possible, and then with furrowed brows we pressed on.

This main road was wider as we went through what once was a bustling town in the mid-1800s. The tiny mountain community I have been a part of my entire life is full of proud people. We passed houses well over 100 years old, yet the paint was fresh, the lawns immaculate . . . even the scattered mobile homes were well maintained with manicured lawns.

We traveled passed a house with a deck, and under the deck appeared to be a giant. I told my husband to slow down, as I fixated my eyes on a large German Shepherd, almost identical to one my husband and I had years ago, but this one was different.

Although she was huge for a female, her head nearly touched the ground as if she was defeated, almost depressed.

On each leg of the move, I made my husband drive back by the house for further investigation. This beautiful animal was under a deck in the muddy holes she probably dug to keep cool the previous summer. She didn't have a house, food, or even water within reach. After several passes, I noticed she had not moved, and if she were lying down instead of standing, I would have taken her for dead. I realized then she was tied to the tree next to the deck. A 90-pound animal tethered by five feet of clothing line cable. My heart sank.

That was the end of my sleep. For the next month, my days were consumed with packing and unpacking, cleaning and painting. My nights were spent researching local and state tethering laws. While searching the Internet, I found Dogs Deserve Better. On June 6th, I emailed Kristi Campbell at DDB information. Her reply explained DDB's dog rescue and outreach. I provided Kristi with the chained dog's address and a pamphlet and letter was mailed from the home office.

I continued to check on this poor animal daily. It was June 18th when I could take no more. I contacted my county's animal control.

The officer explained that he notified the dog's caretakers of the law and told them the situation was unacceptable. They were warned if they did not comply, the animal would be removed, and they could face charges. By June 20th, the homeowner attempted to cure the problem. Their remedy was nothing more than a small plastic igloo type doghouse thrown under the deck.

"That's it," I thought, "As Mikhail Gorbachev said, 'if not me, who? If not now, when?'"

On June 29th, I applied to become a Dogs Deserve Better rep and was approved on July 2nd. My first order of business was to send my own letter and brochure to this residence.

On July 10th, the dog was gone! I rushed to call the animal control officer, and learned he had returned to the home to inform them that they had not complied with the law. They choose to voluntarily surrender the girl and two cats to boot!

The German Shepherd who haunted my days and nights had been saved! My first chained dog, the one who broke my heart daily, had been saved in a month!

Two days later, on July 12th, a volunteer at the shelter contacted me. The precious, currently safe German Shepherd—now well fed, bathed, and brushed—had shown aggression to cats at the shelter. They were going to put her to sleep on July 13th. The same lump that disappeared just two days prior suddenly began sprouting to life again.

On the morning of July 13th, I called the Sheriff's Office requesting a 'stay of execution' because I was on my way to pick her up. I had Hokie transferred to DDB and introduced her to my pack of six.

Since that day, she has put on weight, sleeps on the bed, and lounges on the couch in the AC. For eight years, this dog survived winter storms, frozen nights, spring rains, and summer heat tied to a tree; but in one month, you cannot distinguish her from the rest of our pack—all of who have never slept one single night outside.

I felt empowered by the life I had saved! In the following month, I rescued and adopted out four more dogs. I am currently fostering two rescues. I drove a leg of a transport for five dogs, who spent the night with us in their travels from South Carolina to New York. I have four surrenders awaiting placement in foster or adoptive homes. I have mailed out dozens of brochures.

Hokie the German Shepherd reminds me daily of my purpose by simply cuddling on the bed with me, as if that had been her plan all along. Perhaps she orchestrated the events at the shelter presuming I would bring her home. She does appear self-satisfied and content to be here. Choosing a dog for your family is exciting; to have a dog choose you as her family is simply amazing.

Misha's Story:
from Junkyard to Boardroom

BY DICK CHEATHAM, SUBMITTED BY PAM CHEATHAM, DDB GEORGIA REP

&

Misha poses with Dick for the Bank Annual Report

My wife first met Misha in a junkyard on Luckie Street in downtown Atlanta. She had visited Misha for about four years on her lunch hour jog. Misha's caretaker let her breed with a large black dog, Shadow, twice a year. She had her puppies in the back seats of junked cars. My wife tried talking the guardian into spaying Misha, to no avail.

When my wife noticed that Misha looked sick, she inquired with the junk yard owner about her health. He told my wife that Misha was dying and he was going to put her down. My wife asked him to give her the dog and she took the dog to our vet. She had heartworms.

We started the six week treatment for heartworms and since Misha couldn't be very active during that period, I took her to work with me every day so she could recover and relax in my office. I worked in a bank in Conyers; it wasn't a very happy environment.

Over time I noticed that the employees seemed to change their behavior because of the dog, and they began to interact with each other differently. Misha brought the best out of those people and we had zero turnover for three years in our department while the rest of the bank turned over at a rate in excess of 35% per year.

The President of the bank said that his only complaint about our department was that our morale was too high.

During Misha's tenure at the bank, she broke up two attempted robberies. Office robberies are more common between Thanksgiving and Christmas, and typically thieves will target a small office, one with five or fewer people, and in a single story facility. The reason for this is that there are fewer variables to control and you can see everybody.

On one occasion, two unknown men entered our facility with the intent of sweeping through and collecting wallets and purses. Misha could always sense when something or somebody didn't have the best intentions and she would start growling and barking.

The perpetrators were thrown off rhythm and elected to leave our office because a crazy, threatening dog was another variable that was disruptive and difficult to control. We called the police immediately and they visited our office for an incident report. When we described the characters and their vehicle, the police told us that they had been looking for these guys all over town.

On another occasion, a man under the influence of drugs tried to push his way into our office. I assume it was drugs because his pupils were so dilated you could have shot a basketball through the pupil without touching the iris. Misha backed him out of the building where he stood on the other side of our glass front door, holding it shut to keep Misha away from him. He left before the sheriff arrived.

The Sheriff's Department conducted crisis training for the entire bank and, on one occasion, simulated a robbery in the Main Branch office. Misha reacted appropriately—barking, growling and lunging. Even when it was just a simulation she knew how to react. She was doing her job in protecting her human co-workers.

I would interview prospective employees with Misha. The bank interviewed a lender for a new office we intended to open north of Conyers. Everyone liked the candidate, but Misha was uncomfortable with him. He turned down our offer because he intended to start his own bank in the area.

He did open a bank a year later. After our bank sold I interviewed with that bank and with that individual. They intended to hire me but with the condition that I wouldn't bring the dog. I didn't care for that ultimatum so I didn't pursue the opportunity. Six months after the bank opened, that same man was asked to leave the bank because of poor lending practices. Misha obviously had great instincts about this guy when others didn't.

Our bank was later sold to a group headquartered many miles away and our department was eliminated as part of the acquisition. That was okay because Misha had worked hard for a long time and she is now retired. She goes to department reunions but most of her time is spent doing what she really enjoys—chasing chipmunks and rabbits and splashing in water.

Most people have been around good dogs during their lifetime. A few of us have spent time with a great dog. I will treasure my every moment spent with Misha and am honored that I spent time with one of the great ones; one who almost died at the end of a chain.

Unchained
by Melody

BY MELODY WHITWORTH, DDB MISSOURI REP

༺

Scooby and Melody in the yard

It was October, and I was in the quaint, historical city of Hillsboro, Illinois, for my husband's high school reunion. We were on our way to a gathering at a cottage on the lake when I noticed, visible in plain sight, a dog chained to a tree. I screamed, "STOP!" Before the vehicle came to a complete halt, my door was open and I was on my way to see if the dog was okay.

This was not just any dog, not just any tree and not just any chain. This was a purebred Collie with a logging chain around his neck that was wrapped around a 4-foot tree. The beautiful old tree had two-inch dig marks in its bark; the collie had the chain wrapped around his neck attached with not one, but two padlocks to secure it.

I approached the dog who just lay next to the tree looking at me, depressed, shut down, and broken in spirit. His fur was gray with dirt; the mats in his fur were huge and lay in clumps across his back. He had a cracked, plastic doghouse he was too big for, and water, but no food. All of a sudden I spied a man come out of the house and look at me curiously.

"Is he alright?" I asked.

"He was this morning," the man replied.

"Don't you think it's odd for a stranger to walk up to a dog and the dog doesn't respond, doesn't even get up or bark?"

He didn't reply, but just stood there looking at the dog.

"This is no life for a dog," I persisted.

"Nope, its not," the man agreed. "You want him?"

"Well, I'd like to find him a better home. I'm not in a position to take him this minute; could I come back in the morning?"

"Yep, that'd be fine." He answered.

I couldn't believe it! This seemed just too easy. I was excited and anxious the rest of the day and couldn't wait for the next morning to arrive so I could pick him up. I did not have any of the paperwork required by Dogs Deserve Better for a surrender, so I went to the local newspaper office and asked one of the writers if they could print a release form for me from the website. With heart-thumping success within reach and the appropriate paperwork in hand, I was nervous and on my way to pick up the collie.

When I arrived, the man came out of his house and luckily he carried with him the keys to the padlocks. He agreed to sign the release form and told me that the collie had not been to a vet since he was a pup. While having a brief conversation with the man, I learned the dog's name was Scooby; he was 4-1/2 years old and had been chained to that very tree since he was six months old.

"I bought him for my young son, but the dog proved to be too much of a handful." Scooby's guardian explained.

After releasing him from the chain and placing an appropriate collar and leash on him, I decided to walk him a little to give him some relief before making the three-hour journey back home. Suddenly I heard a familiar voice yell, "Get back in the truck! Now! Get back in the truck!" I looked toward our truck where my husband was urging me to get in and get in quick!

Seems like the woman of the house was not in agreement with finding Scooby a new home and she was quite upset. With my husband's assistance, we hastily coaxed Scooby in the enclosed back, got in quickly ourselves, and sped off. My paperwork was signed and in my pocket. "Sayonara! He's mine now! "

Scooby was very anxious and barked almost the entire three-hour trip. We stopped to let him relieve himself at a gas station and I was afraid I would be arrested for animal abuse because of his condition.

Like most rescuers traveling with a recently liberated animal, I was humiliated by his condition and wished I had a sign that read, "Rescued Dog—I didn't do this to him—I would never treat an animal like this!" I felt defensive and was ready with a verbal response to anyone, "I just rescued him, really!"

Scooby was treated to a professional grooming, vetted, neutered, nourished with high quality food, and received lots of love and patience in our home while he was being fostered.

To add joy to an already-happy ending, a "forever" family adopted Scooby. The beautiful couple is absolutely in love with him and Scooby reciprocates that affection. Mike and Rhonda, his adoptive parents, understand and embrace his breed, personality and even his quirks.

Scooby has a life and a job now: to be Rhonda's companion when her husband Mike has training and active duty with the Army, and he couldn't be happier.

Scooby with Melody and his new family, Mike and Rhonda

A Chained Couple
and Two Chihuahuas

BY AMANDA GREEN, DDB NEW MEXICO REP

℘

One day I received a call from a woman named Stacy who had a six-year-old chained female Pit Bull who had become aggressively protective of her ten-day-old puppies. This was her third litter of puppies while living chained out in the extremely hot or cold temperatures of Southeast New Mexico. Stacy wanted me to take the female but let her keep the puppies. I told her, "No way—if I'm taking the female, I'm taking the puppies."

We set up a time for me to come over to take pictures.

When I arrived to take pictures, this "protective" red brindle female with honey-colored eyes greeted me with a big smile and a wagging tail. I guess they had let her off her chain to take care of her ten puppies on the dirt floor of a rickety carport that also stored a car and lawn mowers. But sure enough to the left of the carport was her thick collar attached to a heavy chain staked to the ground.

In order for us to take a look at the puppies, she chained her up but even then she was not bothered by our presence near the puppies.

The puppies were red brindle and white or fawn brindle and white. I shuddered to think what kind of a home they would receive through a 'for sale' ad in our local paper.

Also on the property chained behind the carport was an extremely handsome six-year-old male Albino Pit Bull Terrier. An extremely-white dog, no pigmented skin, out in the blistering New Mexico sun . . . not a good thing. He also was wearing a thick collar attached to a heavy chain which was staked into the ground. He did have a dog house and a piece of wood that appeared to provide him some shade when the sun was directly overhead.

He had a growth on the skin around his penis and really scabby areas around his eyes. He was really shy and would not let me pet him, but I didn't hold that against him because dogs tend to blossom once they are off the chain and into a home setting.

Apparently this couple of dogs had been a breeding pair over the last six years. The male was the husband's dog who he was "very attached to" and Stacy didn't know if he would give him up. She had also 'found' two of the cutest Chihuahua puppies I had seen in a long time. She was keeping them in a bathroom in her house because her children were too rough with them, and I hoped she'd release them too.

I went ahead and took photos in case they'd release all the dogs to me, and I later got the thumbs up phone call from Stacy: all the dogs would be coming to Dogs Deserve Better.

I got to work building their "freedom fund." If I were to rescue them, I'd need a temporary place for them to board and wanted to raise some vet money too. Within about a week's time, using networking available through Facebook, I had the funding I needed to rescue them.

Ava and her puppies got a week's rest in a boarding facility before going up to Colfax Pet Rescue in Miami, New Mexico. Ava was a very appreciative dog who enjoyed her breaks of belly rubs away from the pups, and I hope that her "belly rub" future is only beginning, that she will have a chance to blossom into someone's loving companion.

Sergio and Hugo, the two Chihuahua brothers, were sent to a DDB-approved foster home in De Pere, Wisconsin, with a lovely couple named June and Bill Smet. I am happy to report that both puppies were all too quickly adopted into loving families.

Ari, the albino male Pit Bull, was fostered at our home for over two months while he received veterinary care for the basal cell carcinoma on the prepuce of his penis area. He also had suffered from so many sun burns around his eyes, that he has severe solar dermatitis and must take a Vitamin A capsule every day for the rest of his life. His skin will probably never recover.

His faith in people, however, blossomed the moment we took him off the chain and allowed him to be what he knew he was meant to be. My heart overflows with love after spending time with Ari.

He has made himself at home with us and other than some minor housetraining issues, he has been extremely easy to be with. I will never forget the lesson he has taught me, that I still have much work to do to help get other dogs like him off chains and into the hearts of their families. For now, until he is adopted or space is made for him in rescue, he will be our dog to love and to cherish until death do us part.

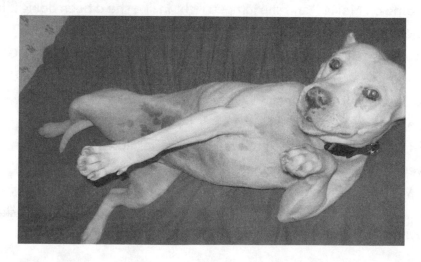

Mollie,
The Glamour Girl

BY ROSE GORDON, DDB ADOPTER & DAWN ASHBY, DDB ILLINOIS REP

℘

I was giving the pugs, Elvis and Simba, baths because they were little stinky dogs. Mollie kept coming in the bathroom and hanging her head into the tub. When I was finished bathing the Pugs I said, "Come on Mollie!" and she jumped right in like she'd been doing it her whole life. She sat there good as gold while Mommy gave her a good scrubbing, shampooing and conditioning with the pugs' Blonde Glam shampoo (even though as a big black Lab she will never be blonde or exceedingly glam). But she will shine at the pool party for dogs we're attending tomorrow!

Mollie's life didn't used to be about parties and glamour girl make-over's though . . . it was anything BUT glamorous.

When Dawn Ashby welcomed this eleven-year-old black Lab, fresh off a chain, into her home to foster, her husband immediately asked, "What are your intentions with this dog?" She stuttered for a second then answered, "I'm going to adopt her out of course." She secretly smiled, never dreaming she'd find a home for the old girl who'd spent her life on a chain and was plagued by a tumor that hung down and swung from under her front leg.

I saw Mollie on the Dogs Deserve Better Petfinder site and contacted Dawn. I had been missing having a Black Lab in my home since the passing of my last, and was ready to be an angel to another rescue dog.

Dawn's reply email was a story she published in the Dogs Deserve Better newsletter about Mollie's life on a chain and her first bath, the "glamour treatment" at the groomer. I cried when I learned of Mollie's previous life and immediately wanted to adopt her. I didn't care about her age, in fact, it made me want to adopt her even more—to give her the life she'd never had a chance to know.

Dawn's daughter, Michelle, lived near my St. Louis, Missouri residence, and so we arranged for Dawn to bring Mollie for a home visit and to meet my husband Gary and I.

It was obvious to Dawn and Michelle from the beginning that we intended to provide a loving inside home for Mollie. Still Dawn would not let herself get her hopes up about the adoption. She felt it was too good to be true that Mollie's humble beginnings would lead to a fairytale ending. I don't know what she was so worried about, how could we have possibly resisted Mollie's charm?

Mollie has made a lot of new friends and experienced many adventures since moving home with us. Early after her adoption, Gary was in the front yard with her when something caught his attention. He turned for a brief moment and when he turned back around, Mollie was gone. "Where could an eleven-year-old Lab disappear to so quickly?" He wondered.

He began walking down the sidewalk searching for her. He spied Mollie playing dress-up with some little neighbor girls a couple doors down. As he drew closer, he noticed Mollie had been accessorized with a lovely pink scarf. She was heading inside through the front door with her new little friends when Gary called for her saying, "Mollie, playtime is over. Tell your friends goodbye. It's time to go home."

Isn't that just like a typical dad, always ruining a girl's fun?

We took Mollie to the vet to remove all her tumors and growths, which were many. After surgery, she looked like the dog from Tim Burton's short film "Frankenweenie" with the way she was stitched together. For us, it was well worth it to keep her in good health, as we are hoping for as much time as possible with our angel.

Many chained dogs are found neglected and emaciated, but Mollie was overweight due to lack of exercise and a constant diet of cheap dry dog food being dumped out on the ground for her.

Now Mollie is on a healthy diet, going for walks, playing ball in the yard, wading in her little kiddy pool and sometimes she gets to play with other dogs during "Doggie Swim Parties" at local pools. She and her Pug brother and sister also play catch the little Doxie pup when my sister comes to visit with her puppy mill rescue. Mollie, Elvis and Simba run around and around the house in hot pursuit with their little Doxie cousin calling out "Catch me if you can!"

Mollie's history is a lot like that of other chained dogs, except she's lucky enough to have the happy ending that many don't get. A woman knew of Mollie living in a nearby town and asked Dawn to help her. Dawn visited the provided address where she spoke with Mollie's guardian, left a card with her number, and a Dogs Deserve Better educational brochure.

On occasion she would visit Mollie and her guardian, initiate small talk and bring treats for Mollie. Such visits served as a reminder of her interest in Mollie's well being. Dawn was experienced in dealing with caretakers of chained backyard dogs. By supplying Mollie's guardian with her contact information, establishing a good rapport, and providing an open-ended offer of assistance, Mollie's rescue had been set in motion.

As predicted, the day arrived when Mollie became an inconvenience and Dawn was called on her offer to help. Mollie's caregiver and family purchased a new home in a nice subdivision where chained dogs weren't allowed.

Surprisingly, Mollie's guardian felt obligated to visit his vet to update her vaccinations before turning her over to Dawn. On the day of her vet visit, he stopped by Dawn's home with Mollie riding inside a kennel strapped in the back of his pick-up truck. Dawn requested Mollie be let out and brought into the house to become acquainted with the surroundings. Her guardian hesitated.

"Mollie's an outside dog." He explained.

"If she comes here, she will be an inside dog. We don't believe in outside dogs. All dogs are equal here. All dogs deserve to be part of the family." Dawn told him.

"I've had her since she was a puppy and she's never been housebroken and she's always lived outside," he persisted.

"It's OK, I'll train her," she assured him.

"You can do that now at her age? After she's lived outdoors all her life?" He asked.

She explained by presenting her personal experience, "It's easier to housetrain an older dog than a puppy. I find dogs who never had the opportunity to live in the house tend to be appreciative and eager to learn and please. Of course she'll have a few accidents. I have good cleaners for that. She'll basically housebreak herself when she understands what I want from her."

Mollie was reluctant to go through the front door and needed a boost, a fear-based reaction which is common for a dog who's never been allowed inside. Mollie sat in the sunroom while Dawn spoke softly, gently petting her. Mollie's guardian handed over the vet records. He discussed Mollie's tumor explaining how his vet told him it was benign and not a problem.

Mollie didn't stay that day. Her guardian promised to follow up in a few days with a phone call.

Dawn sprayed the sunroom with air freshener, but Mollie's unpleasant odor lingered. She freshened the air while thinking how desperately Mollie needed a bath.

Dawn replayed the events of the day in her mind, trying to remember anything out of the ordinary. She suspected something put off Mollie's caregiver, but what? She had hoped Mollie would stay, so what went wrong? She was concerned. Did something happen to change his mind? She was right to worry.

A few days later she received a phone call as promised. The guardian's apprehension was caused by his doubt that an outside dog could be trained to live indoors. He was certain once Dawn was unable to train Mollie, she would call him to take her back and he didn't know what he'd do with her then.

After he left Dawn's house that day he contacted his father, attempting to convince him to take Mollie. Why couldn't he chain her up in that old barn on his farm? His dad refused. He didn't have time to tromp out to the barn to feed and water a dog.

Dawn pulled up the drive in front of a garage packed with moving boxes filled with items the family couldn't part with. They must have spent days carefully packing the possessions they had to move with them. Boxes full of stuff no one wanted to get rid of, material possessions loved or needed too much for the family to live without. Those objects considered too valuable to toss away, too expensive to replace, or too important to trade or give away when they moved into their new home.

After eleven years, Mollie wasn't one of those things.

Dawn walked into the backyard where she found Mollie tethered to a tree instead of chained in her usual spot by her doghouse. Mollie had been for a long walk around the neighborhood, her guardian's parting gift to her. He shed tears as he confessed he should have treated Mollie better, should have taken her for more walks like that one. Before Dawn could be touched by his emotion, a yapping from within the house diverted her attention.

"You have another dog?" she asked.

"We have a little inside dog for the kids." He replied.

Mollie looked up at Dawn and rolled her eyes.

"We'll just get out of your way. I know you're busy with the move."

"You're sure you won't be needing Mollie's doghouse or chain or anything?" He offered.

"Positive." She replied.

Then Dawn opened the passenger door to her truck cab and said "Mollie Up!"

Whether this was a common command Mollie understood or only because she is an incredibly cool dog who knows how to make a memorable exit, Mollie immediately jumped in the truck on cue. Then with a big finish she flipped her tail straight up to the window where her guardian stood and with her tail standing straight in the air she flipped him the bird Mollie style!

They rode with the windows down so Mollie wouldn't be self-conscience of her stench. On the way they stopped at a drive-thru for a celebration treat for Mollie, which she in turn upchucked in Dawn's lap.

At the Ashby's, Dawn immediately made it a point to call dog grooming services until she found one with an opening the following day. A unanimous family vote decided Mollie smelled too rancid to be allowed to sleep in the house. Mollie had to spend her first night of freedom sleeping in a garage with access to a fenced backyard.

However, this time Mollie didn't spend the night alone. Dawn dug out her sleeping bag, and, dragging her pillow and blankets behind her, she set up camp in the garage with Mollie.

Turns out though, that Dawn and Mollie weren't alone either, because anywhere Dawn goes, the other dogs follow. An impromptu doggie slumber party celebrated Mollie's arrival to freedom!

The next day Dawn drove Mollie to Fairview Heights, Illinois, for her grooming appointment, where she received "The Star Treatment" grooming package.

Mollie went from her first bath—maybe EVER—out of pure necessity, to her most recent bath in her own bathtub, in her own family home, given by her own mommy's loving hands.

Oh, Mollie, dahling, you look Fab-u-lous!

It's all About Teamwork

BY MONICA ALCORN, DDB INDIANA REP
CAROLYN LINDSAY, DDB INDIANA REP
WITH MARIE BELANGER, DDB NATIONAL REP COORDINATOR, INDIANA

§

Part I of II

BY MONICA ALCORN

It was my first rescue as a newly appointed representative for Dogs Deserve Better. I received a desperate call from Marie Belanger, the National Rep Coordinator, asking if there was any way I could take in six puppies and possibly the mother. She emphasized there was no time to waste. If you know me you know that the word "no" rarely, if ever, comes out of my mouth. It is my passion to rescue animals and I sometimes find myself a little overwhelmed, but I love taking part in rescue.

I am an animal control officer for my city so it happens quite often that I'm helping people in my community find homes for their dogs or I take in hard luck cases which wouldn't have a chance anywhere else. My boyfriend has always been there (sometimes whether he likes it or not), helping me care for animals, interview potential adopters at home visits, or run to the vet, and all the other fun stuff he hasn't quite learned to appreciate yet.

In some ways we are very different and he has no trouble at all saying the word "no"; he can get quite frustrated with me when I don't. He has laid down one rule for me, well tried to anyway, and that rule is "NO PUPPIES!!!! Ever!!"

So, when Marie called me it was my gut instinct to say "YES" but in the back of my head I knew I would be getting myself in trouble at home. I swear I was shaking my head "NO" while I was on the phone with Marie, but I heard a strange voice come out of my mouth saying, "YES!"

I don't suppose my boyfriend would believe it was some sort of demonic possession, would he? Temporary insanity?

Carolyn (another DDB volunteer with a huge heart) transported the six pups and the momma to my house. I went out and bought a 4x4x6 kennel and transformed my kitchen into a puppy room (sort of like a baby's room for puppies). I was so excited! After getting everyone settled in it was time for me to go to work.

My boyfriend and I work opposite shifts. It was about this time that I was questioning whether he would be as mutually enthusiastic when he walked in after work to find a kitchen full of dogs.

Because I do my best thinking when backed into a corner I came up with a brilliant plan. I decided to lessen the blow by writing a letter to him from the dog! I wrote him a note from the momma dog thank-ing him for taking her and the pups in and giving them all a second chance at the life they deserve. I signed it momma dog and drew a paw print. Then I waited.

My phone rang at 6:15 p.m., right on time. I reluctantly answered and he said, "Where did all these dogs come from?" I answered hon-estly with "I don't know." No, really. I had forgotten the name of the city that Carolyn had picked them up in so I didn't know.

Plus, I was trying desperately to add some humor to the volatile situation.

I explained to him the pitiful life the momma dog had led. She spent all six years of her life on a chain or in a dirty pen outside. In that miserable and lonely six years she had seven litters of puppies!! The people weren't even breeding her for money. They were advertising these precious pups for free on the internet and were just too lazy to get her fixed!

I admit I laid it on pretty thick in hopes that he'd still be living there when I got home from work. Even more importantly, I was hoping I'd still be living at all once I got home from work!

The first night was pretty miserable as the puppies cried all night. But they learned quickly that they were in a safe place and have been sleeping through the night since. They are the cutest little things and momma dog is always on her best behavior!

It has been eleven days as I write and three of the puppies have been spoken for, plus the momma dog too! I'm just waiting to have them altered and chipped before going to their new homes.

I am thankful to Marie and Carolyn for finding out about these great dogs and getting them to me. I'm especially grateful to my amazingly wonderful and understanding boyfriend who I appreciate more than words can say for accepting the pups and learning that they aren't so bad after all. (Yep, I'll be spreading it a little thick for a good a while.)

I look forward to many more successful rescue stories as a rep for Dogs Deserve Better. I am very proud to be part of such a great group.

Carly while still on her chain in the backyard

Part II of II

BY CAROLYN LINDSAY

Now that you've read the end of Carly and her puppies' story, I want to fill you in on the beginning. I'm Carolyn Lindsay and this is how Carly and her six puppies became another Dog Deserve Better rescue success.

I was searching an online classified site—I do this every few nights—looking for 'free to good home ads' and trying to educate people who don't understand the dangers of such ads or confronting those who could care less and want rid of their castoff pets.

Dog bunchers, devious people who collect free dogs and take

them out of state to dog auctions where they are sold for laboratory use, dog fighting, or other money making opportunities, scour the classifieds looking for free dogs to pick up. Sometimes they even go so far as to bring their children and spouses with them, posing as a loving family. The majority of people fall for it.

One woman in Advance, Indiana, had a free to good home ad for six puppies. I'll be honest and tell you these kinds of ads really anger me. I sent her an article and was very blunt with my opinion to say the least, asking her to please take the ad down. She replied with a rude letter pretty much telling me to mind my own business. What she doesn't understand is that when it comes to animals I make it my business, because they don't have a voice to speak for themselves. They need the help of compassionate people to protect them.

I then decided to swallow my pride and write her an apology letter, persuasive in nature, hoping she would give the dogs to me rather than risk them ending up in the hands of some conniving deviant.

I contacted Marie attaching the email of the advertisement. She told me that she might have a foster to take them in. Marie bragged about a gem of a woman, a new rep, Monica Alcorn, a city animal control officer who also works for a vet. When I spoke with Monica she agreed to take them, but I had to get the pups to her.

I spoke with the ad poster on the phone. She said I could have the puppies, but warned me the mother was in terrible condition. I immediately saw a red flag go up. "Why is the mother in such terrible condition?" I asked. She explained the dog was six years old and this was her seventh litter of pups. "She's very skinny," is all she told me.

I had to bite my lip to keep from reaching through the phone and choking her. Reminding myself to breathe, I managed to remain calm. I drove to her home and in the back yard I saw the puppies and the mother. I almost cried. My nephew was with me and he did cry.

Carly was so emaciated her hip bones protruded three inches and her waist was no more then four inches across. Her left ear had a large sore from fly strikes. She was on a chain. There was no water or food for her.

I gathered the six puppies from the muddy dirt pit and loaded them into my car. Then I approached the woman and asked if I she would please release the mother to me. She first said no because her husband had warned her that when he got home the dog had better be there.

She told me she and her husband were thinking of euthanizing her because they figured she had cancer or something. She'd never seen a vet in her life.

Once again, I firmly laid it out straight, "Looking at the shape she's in, your dog is probably going to die anyway, and then you won't have her either way."

She not only agreed with my assessment, she agreed to let me take the dog. Without a moment's hesitation, I loaded her up in the car along with her puppies.

The whole way to Monica's house Carly stood in between the seats kissing me, "Thank you, thank you," radiating throughout her entire being. She was so sweet and the puppies were beautiful—one female and five males—two blondes, one looked like a little wolf, and the rest were gold and black.

When I arrived at Monica's she was happy to see them. She bought a crate and we set it up in the kitchen. The puppies were happy to be out of dirt and little momma Carly loved being indoors and receiving love and attention.

Carly ate while in my car, ate again when she arrived at Monica's, and then she pulled a bag of dog food out of a sack and was wanting to eat that too! It was obvious she was starving!

It's only going to get better for Carly and her babies. Carly will never have another litter of puppies and she can live her own life to love, be loved, and never feel the pangs of hunger again. She will sleep inside on her own pillow with her own family to love her. They will see the beauty in Carly that her original guardians selfishly missed.

The puppies will be neutered and spayed then adopted into inside forever homes where they will never have to go through what their mother endured. It was an exhausting, but oh-so-good day for rescue. Carly is free to run, to play, and most importantly, will never be chained again.

One of Carly's puppies, looking forward to his new life

All I Want for Christmas
is One Wild and Crazy Dog

BY PATRICIA ALDERING, DDB MICHIGAN REP

❧

Cody's story is one which touched many people in my community and made them realize chaining a dog is not the answer. He was one of my first rescues, and the fact that his rescue occurred at Christmas-time made it even more special to me. He was my gift.

I had been a DDB rep for about five months when I started receiving information on him from concerned citizens who drove by him every day. Callers described him as a Husky or White Shepherd, chained outside a big red barn. They stated he had been there for years and that he appeared lonely and bored.

It was the week before Christmas, a typical cold and snowy Michigan night. One of my volunteers, Sarah, and I decided to stop and talk to the guardian. We pulled into the driveway and a man approached us. I introduced myself and told him I was with Dogs Deserve Better. I asked why the dog was chained and he responded by saying Cody was a crazy-wild dog. Obviously, I thought this meant he was mean and aggressive and I contemplated whether I should approach him.

The man was cordial, which in and of itself is unusual when dealing with chained dog caretakers. He was soft-spoken and I did not feel threatened by him, unlike other chained dog guardians I've meet, who've been downright nasty and intimidating.

I explained to the man I was concerned about Cody's psychological health. I pointed out that Cody was pacing and that was a sign he had psychologically "lost it," he was losing his mind. The man was hearing what I was saying. I could tell he was pondering my words. He proceeded to tell me the story behind Cody.

Cody had been a puppy when dumped at his house 12 years earlier and he brought him into his home. Cody proceeded to tear apart his house and thus Cody wound up on the chain. The man said Cody did have a nice warm place in the barn, and I could see that his chain reached inside the barn. He unyieldingly told me he would not bring Cody back into the house.

I said I would be willing to take Cody and find him a good home. I could tell he was considering my words, but he said he wanted to think it over and also discuss it with his wife. I gave him a DDB brochure with my number on it.

Sarah and I returned to the car and left. Over the next week, I would lie in bed and tell myself that all I wanted for Christmas was for Cody to be off that chain. That was the only Christmas present I desired. I thought about him day and night.

The week after Christmas, Cody's guardian contacted me. He said I was right, Cody deserved a better home, and yes, he and his wife decided I could come get him. I contacted one of my volunteers, Therese, to ask her if she could keep Cody overnight. My husband

Randy and I were heading out of town early the next morning and we could not keep Cody that night. Therese agreed and Cody arrived at her house later that evening, accompanied by a crate, for I hadn't forgotten the words his guardian told me earlier: "Cody tore apart my house, so I had to chain him outside."

Cody was extremely dirty and Thereses' husband Kurt offered to bathe him. I was concerned because Cody's previous guardian had mentioned Cody was a crazy-wild dog. I had images in my head of Kurt walking out of the bathroom in shreds, covered in blood. Kurt didn't seem worried as he and Cody trotted away. Therese and I chatted in the kitchen. I was tense; listening for screams to come from the bathroom where Cody was being bathed.

Shortly thereafter, Kurt and Cody emerged from the bathroom. They were both wet, but Kurt was unscathed, and both Cody and Kurt had smiles on their faces. Everything had gone smoothly. Cody spent the night with Kurt and Therese, and when we picked him up the next day, Kurt referred to him as a gentle giant.

It took Cody many weeks off the chain before he stopped pacing. When loose in our yard I would catch him pacing in a half circle. It was all he knew.

A month after his rescue Cody's previous caregivers contacted me wanting to know how Cody was doing. I told them he was doing fine. I could tell, in their hearts, they felt very bad for keeping him chained. They told me they were holding onto the DDB brochure and they were going to pass it along to the caretaker of the next chained dog they saw. I usually have no respect for chained dog owners, in fact most I downright detest. But there was something about Cody's guardians; I had a certain amount of respect for them. They had sincerely admitted what they had done was wrong and not ONCE did they make me feel guilty for stopping by their house to talk to them about their dog. Because they listened and believed in what I was saying, their dog was given a better life.

Ironically, I had been trying to get one of their neighbors' dog off the chain, but I never approached them personally. I was mailing them DDB literature and heard rumors another rescue group had stopped by to speak with them and were unsuccessful in rescuing the dog.

After Cody's rescue, I never saw the dog on the chain again, but I have seen him wandering the large property. I will always wonder if Cody's owners passed along that brochure.

Cody was not the worse case scenario; he was fed, licensed, and given heartworm pills. The most terrible part for Cody was his collar was too tight and rubbed his neck raw, his ears showed damage from fly bites and his years on the chain did affect him mentally.

As for being a wild and crazy dog—NOT! He is the most laid-back, gentle dog who loves plush toys even though he will take them apart. Who cares? They are his toys to do what he wants with. He was just being a puppy when he tore the previous guardian's house apart. Untrained, undisciplined puppies do that.

Cody, stuck on a chain, had not been given another chance to show his guardians what a great dog he could grow into. Don't we all calm down as we grow older?

Cody's guardians claimed he was 12 years old, but my veterinarian said he appeared closer to eight. Guardians of chained dogs often tell us their dogs are older than they are. It's a mystery as to why, but we believe given the sparse attention they pay to the dogs, they just plum forget when they arrived.

We have determined him to be a Yellow Lab mixed with Shepherd or Husky. By the way, why do I know so much about Cody? Because my family was so attached to him we could not part with him. Three years later, he is still with us.

Several of the people who contacted me about Cody are still in his life. They hold fundraisers; donate much needed dog items, and occasionally stop by my house to pay the gentle giant a visit. Therese and her young daughters visit Cody and take him for walks.

Three years ago I made a Christmas wish for a dog described as wild and crazy. A week later, my wish came true. At the time, I had no idea Cody would still be with me today. He is part of my family, a gift who continues to give.

Don't Worry, Be Happy
Griffie's Song

BY GAYLA HAUSMAN, DDB NEBRASKA REP

ℰ

Gayla and Griffie taking a stroll

I can't say I was surprised to be asked to take in a chained dog from the small town of Blue Springs, Nebraska. It appeared as though every dog in this borough was chained or penned. Most every house was in need of TLC, paint chipping off the facade, porches dilapidated, broken down vehicles junked in the yards, and the dog pens were littered with debris. It was the first time I'd visited, but doubted it would be my last.

It's more common in unfortunate areas to see dogs left outside for life, but it really has nothing to do with money. Housebreaking and a collar and leash for walks costs less than a chain and a doghouse.

Some say laziness explains why people who rarely take care of themselves don't properly care for their homes or pets. I guess that could be true, or perhaps people who make bad choices for their own lives often make bad choices for their companions too.

Whatever the case, it's an absolute truth that where you see one backyard dog, you're more than likely to find another. Social acceptance plays a major role in chaining a dog for life, which is one reason we at DDB feel we can be successful at ending this form of animal cruelty: when it becomes less accepted in one neighborhood, it will soon be unacceptable in all neighborhoods.

When DDB reps suggest bringing a dog into the house, the reaction is frequently a look of shock, like you just landed in their neighborhood from another planet. Unless the dog will fit in a purse, it's too big to go inside the house. We attempt to create a visual image explaining, "You watch TV, right? (We know they are glued to the TV, so hope that they will put two and two together.) On TV the dogs always live inside."

The response is always the same, "TV isn't real." Seems the more ramshackle the house, the more untidy the inside of the home, the more likely you'll hear property owners say, "Dogs can't live in the house because they're dirty and make too much of a mess."

As we pulled up, we saw him from the street. He was a brindle Boxer mix, barking and lunging at us as even as we got out of our car. He was fixed to a tree by a heavy chain. No collar, just another chain wrapped so tightly around his neck you couldn't get a finger under it. The dirt he lived in was bare of grass, mud when it was wet, and dust when it was dry. He had a doghouse, if you could call it a house.

I guess anything with a roof on it qualifies as adequate shelter. Never mind if it has gaps so big you can put your hand through them, the roof leaks, and it has no bedding. I guess this was supposed to be his house.

His name was Damon then. It reminded me of Demon, so I knew a name change was in order. I always get nervous when I'm about to take a dog off a chain. You never know what you may be getting yourself into. Is he aggressive? Will he get along with the other foster dogs? Does he have any diseases or parasites our dogs will catch? Will I have enough resources to vet him? We have a lot of reps rescuing and funds can only go so far. Have there been enough donations contributed to cover it? What if his vet bill is unbelievably high? Am I equipped to handle whatever baggage comes with this dog? It's just the luck of the draw.

I asked myself, "Do you feel lucky, punk?"

On the other hand, I was equally as worried about what would happen to the dog if I didn't rescue him. What if the guardians change their minds at the last minute and decide not to surrender the dog?

What if I'm told, "I love my dog"? How many times have I heard that? If this is someone's idea of love, the dog is better off without it.

A dog loved by the family would not have been left isolated, lonely, and starving for companionship.

I had no reason to worry. The man told me, "just take him; I won't miss his barking."

So we did…we put him in the back seat of my car. We hadn't driven two blocks when the dog ever so gently climbed up into the passenger seat and put his head on my companion's shoulder. That's where he stayed for the remainder of the 25-minute drive to the vet. He relaxed into Mari's touch, her embrace, and her silent acknowledgment of love. It must have felt good to be held after being deprived of a gentle hand for so long. Silly me, I was worried.

We took him to the vet to be neutered; heartworm tested, and brought up to date on his vaccinations. We stayed with him until he fell asleep, and he was as docile as a lamb.

We picked him up the next day and drove to meet Carol Clark, his foster mom, at her farm in Diller. Carol already had one huge dog and two little dogs, plus some goats, chickens, cows, and a whole lot of cats. I'm not going to say I was worried again, seeing how much energy I wasted needlessly worrying before.

So, hmmm, what's another word for worry?

I fretted over how well the dog would take to Carol's menagerie of animals. Griffie, his new name, adjusted in no time. He was never tied up outside while the family did the chores. He was never penned. He was allowed to run the farm with the other dogs and live inside with his foster family.

From the day Griffie arrived at Carol's house, he never harmed the head of one life—no matter how large or how small. He loved the companionship of the other dogs, and played, ran and wagged that long tail of his until he dropped from exhaustion. Carol was a little like Dr. Dolittle, but more like Elly May Clampett in her way with the critters. She is patient and calm with the strength of two men.

It was my first trip back to Carol's farm to see Griffie. I noticed the instant I saw him there was a color change in Griffie's' coat. Originally, I thought he was brown and black, but he was so filthy we couldn't see the beautiful orange stripes. He smelled much better too.

Regrettably, I learned not all of my worry was in vain. Griffie had been diagnosed with rectal prolapse; it bled off and on, rendering him unadoptable. I could not imagine anyone wanting a dog who bled all over the house. I educated myself on the choice of surgery for him and learned it is not always successful.

What would happen to Griffie if this couldn't be cured? Who would want him as an indoor dog then? Worry, worry, and more worry! Hey now, you'd be concerned in this situation too.

I decided to put my trust in John McCubbin, our vet in Pickrell. During Griffie's physical exam, he could feel a polyp. He wasn't sure he could get to it rectally to remove it, but said it was worth a try. So, try he did and the surgery was a success, no more prolapsed rectum! Now my dear friend Griffie was truly adoptable. I was ready to let my anxiety over Griffie ease away and my nerves begin to settle.

Griffie stayed with me this time. He slept on top of me in my recliner. He shared his big sloppy kisses. He could even walk off leash and was the most obedient dog I've known. Oh, what a diamond in the rough his previous guardian stuck on a chain and then tossed away!

I knew the day would come when Griffie would be adopted. Adoptions are always bittersweet; on one hand, I am happy for the dog in finding his forever home, but on the other, it's so sad to say goodbye. I had developed a strong bond with Griffie—I couldn't imagine never seeing him again. It would have to be a special home for me to let my boy go.

When I met his potential adopter, I could not have been more pleased. She had been searching for her perfect dog for six months. Griffie's story and picture won her over. I invited her to come meet him and it was love at first sight. When we talked, I realized even more how she had been looking for the "'perfect dog." I had always called Griffie the "perfect dog" . . . It was a match made in heaven! Kori was educated in canine psychology and behavior. She bought a new harness and leash, big fluffy dog beds to put around the house, high quality food, and toys . . . lots of toys. When she left that day she cried for joy, literally cried for joy! There was no denying I had found the right home for Griffie. Kori found her perfect dog and Griffie found his perfect human.

A few days later, I opened my email to find this note from her: "I knew I could love an animal this much, but I didn't know he would love me back just as much. He really is the best dog for my husband and me. Thank you so much and take care."

Kori with her "perfect dog"

I let out a deep sob that worked its way up from the pit of my stomach. Griffie wasn't coming back. He was happy and his family was happy. He had the most loving home I could have possibly found for him. I knew that, so why was I sad, why should I worry? My sorrow for my loss turned into a cry of bliss. He was in a home where someone loved him as much as I loved him. Oh, I still miss Griffie, I talk about him a lot—probably too much—but I don't ever worry about him anymore. He is happy, healthy, and thanks to Kori and her husband Dan, he has a home of his own and the gift of their love.

Emma Emerges Victorious—
A Super Bowl Save

BY AMANDA GREEN, DDB NEW MEXICO REP

ℬ

I first met Emma on Christmas Eve. I was playing Santa delivering presents to chained and penned dogs around Hobbs, New Mexico. The year was approaching its end, monumental to me as my first year serving Dogs Deserve Better.

I had 38 gifts to present to needy backyard dogs. I wished to find the worst of the worst to receive the gifts and ease their suffering, if only temporarily. I knew of a trailer park with a bad reputation as a rough area, and decided this was a good place to start passing out gifts. The hodge-podge mix of chained and penned dogs in the trailer park included a blind dog, two puppies, and a very ferocious dog chained near playing children.

The vicious dog had bitten people before. The dog's negative behavior was reinforced and his rupturing psyche accelerated by constant chaining. The dog was a ticking bomb ready to explode. Fear told me it would only be a matter of time before someone would be seriously injured, more than likely the victim would be an innocent child.

I know all too much about chained dog attacks on children. Dogs Deserve Better keeps an additional site, www.mothersagainstdogchaining.org. Chained dog attacks on children severe enough to be reported by the media are listed there. Family members often recount the incidents for the public to read. The web page also serves as a help group for the parents of the victims. Those parents can privately connect with others who have undergone similar tragedies.

Dogs Deserve Better is unique in that it focuses solely on backyard dogs, but includes all areas of it, and offers many ways to encourage people to keep dogs as members of the family. Dogs Deserve Better often helps pets and their people.

DDB's education outreach, spaying and neutering of rescued pets, careful screening of adopters, fence building for guardians who agree to make their dogs part of the family, and support for parents whose children have been attacked are just a few examples of our commitment to both the dogs and our communities.

The home where Emma lived had four dogs living chained to various stationary objects including cars and trees. They had a Chihuahua, a Pit Bull terrier mix, an American Pit Bull Terrier, and a Pit Bull/ Shepherd mix puppy (Emma). I called animal control the first day he was in after the holidays to ask it he would cite the caretakers for non-potable drinking water on the female American Pit Bull Terrier.

I passed out all the gifts, with guardians' permission, to backyard dogs living lonely, isolated existences. All of the dogs seemed to enjoy their humble Christmas presents. Each received a chew bone, a ball, and two toys. This would be the last time I'd see Emma until Super

Bowl Sunday of the following January.

A local pet supply store, Pet Sense, had provided me with dog food donations, and my husband was out of town for work. I loaded up the dog food, my daughter Savannah, and went to pass out food to people I had made contact with during my backyard dog Christmas gift giving. Emma's was the first home I visited on Super Bowl Sunday.

I pulled up at the trailer at the same time the 'man of the house' arrived home. I gave him a bag of dog food, for which he seemed thankful. I asked if I could visit the dogs. He agreed, saying it would be fine. When I was a foot or so away from Emma I began to smell the stench of infection. It could have just as easily been the odor of feces or the contaminated drinking water left for her, I guessed. I investigated and after closer inspection realized the smell was emanating from Emma's neck. My original presumption had been correct; her neck reeked from an untreated, infected wound.

Emma's cheap, inadequate, and severely tight flea collar had served no other purpose than to cut into her neck. The open wound had allowed skin to heal over the collar. I was in shock as I quickly gathered my thoughts. I had to refocus before I regretted the words I ached to shout at the woman who lived in the home and was headed toward me. I had just spied her as she was rounding the corner of the trailer and walking my way. My temper in check, I spoke to her seriously, yet politely. A negative comment might have alienated me from helping the dog.

I fully intended to beg for Emma's surrender and get her out of this place and to a vet right away. I asked the woman if she knew what had happened to the pup, to which she answered no. I explained the extent of Emma's condition, the embedded collar, and the need for emergency care and asked if I could take Emma. She said she would go down and ask her daughter at another trailer. Emma (then named Mia) was her daughter's dog. I will never forget what she asked me when she returned.

She said, "My daughter said you can have the dog only if you are going to take good care of her." The audacity! It actually caused me to take a step back. Here I find Emma living in pain and torture, isolated on a chain, malnourished, no access to clean drinking water, not to mention no one even noticed the ongoing collar injury, which probably started at least a month ago…and their concern was if I was going to take good care of her?

I thought, "How much worse could anyone care for her?" Instead of voicing my opinion, I shook it off, smiled, and said, "Yes. I am taking her to the vet right now." I hoped my tongue wasn't bleeding from my need to bite into it so hard. My adrenaline was flowing too fast for me to notice the pain.

They did give her up to me, I took her to the emergency vet, and, as horrible as her wound was (we're sparing you the photo), it has healed in time.

Emma has become the poster child for chained dogs in Hobbs, New Mexico, and Lea County. She's an example of the neglect dogs are subjected to when living forgotten at the end of a chain. I've fought with city officials over banning chaining and instead they chose to make the chaining standards more humane by requiring trolley systems and harnesses. But in all actuality, even if Emma had been on a trolley system and had been wearing a harness, she probably still would have suffered the trauma of the neck wound.

It's my firm belief that Emma's life didn't begin the day she was born. Her life began after she was rescued from constant backyard chaining.

The Pittsburgh Steelers were the NFL Super Bowl Champions that year. Here in New Mexico, Dogs Deserve Better was Emma's champion. As a representative for them, I was able to come to her defense, and give her the necessary aid to save her life. Emma emerged victorious from those circumstances.

While America cheered for an NFL team to win, DDB reps cheered

Emma's liberation. With the organization's help she was treated for her wound and fully vetted. She has been adopted to a loving home and enjoys playing with her dog friend Spirit, two cats, and two wonderful people with enough love to give her the home she has always deserved.

I'm already stocking up on supplies to play Santa to needy chained dogs in New Mexico for this year's DDB Christmas Project. I've been purchasing treats and toys to hand out, and I'm taking donations of food and other items for my backyard dog gift collection. I imagine I'll meet new dogs and will be making return visits to them in the coming year. I wonder, who will be the winner this coming Super Bowl? You know I'm not talking football!

I haven't missed the paradox of Emma, the Pit Bull Terrier mix, being rescued on Super Bowl Sunday, and quarterback Michael Vick returning to the NFL to play for the Philadelphia Eagles after chaining, training, torturing and killing Pit Bulls for dog fighting.

I'm so happy that I'm on the Good Guy's side. At least I can sleep at night; I don't know how people like Michael Vick and Emma's caretakers can possibly sleep after causing so much pain.

Isaiah
From Cruelty Case to DDB Cover Dog

BY RHONDA SIMS, FREEDOM TRAIN TRANSPORTS, SOUTH CAROLINA

Rhonda loving up on Isaiah when she sees him again

I was contacted by the local shelter staff about a dog who was on hold for a cruelty case. A neighbor had called Animal control to make a report after no longer being able to look at the pitiful dog who languished inside of his filthy, cramped pen. The dog suffered from starvation, sickness, and blindness in one eye, which the veterinarian later said was due to being kicked in the side of the head.

Although my county has very few animal welfare ordinances to protect the animals who depend so desperately on human kindness, the suffering that was present was such that officers were able to immediately take the dog into custody. He then went to the county animal shelter's holding area, where he would have to remain until

the court case was over. During the hold, I was asked to find placement for him once he was released. I was given a picture of him, and
what I saw made my eyes water and my guts ache.

For there on my computer screen, burning into my very soul, was
a face that I will never forget. One who's eyes possessed no hope or
light, and who's body slumped from the weight of the broken spirit
within. One who had no idea what it was like to be loved, or cared
for; one who had no knowledge of anything other than the horrid
conditions that had plagued his entire existence. Emaciated and bald-
ing, his condition epitomized neglect and abuse.

I named him Isaiah, which means "Salvation by God," because I truly
felt that God saved this helpless creature from his life of misery.

After the court case was over, and the man who had kept Isaiah in
his captivity was ordered never to have another pet again, I was then
able to pull him from the shelter and send him to his safe haven up
north. On my way to the shelter that morning, I was actually anxious
about seeing him, because he reminded me so much of a more pitiful
version of my Charlie. His buff colored coat and sweet eyes played
heavily on my heart, and once again I found myself sobbing as I pulled

through the six foot gates of the shelter driveway.

Inside, I waited as Shead went to the holding area to get him. When she walked through the doorway with him, I was struck by Isaiah's fragility and what seemed to be a staggering weakness. Yet beyond that, I saw a strong will to survive and even thrive. I have always said that I learn my greatest lessons in life from these discarded animals, and I learned an entire textbook of life lessons in that one instant. I reached down and touched Isaiah on the head and his little sparsely furred nub began to wag.

It was my Charlie, only feeble, and I was without words. I picked up Isaiah's slight frame and stood with him in my arms. He seemed to feel secure, and didn't try to get away. At that moment I made him a promise that I would make sure his future was much better than his past, and that I wouldn't let him down.

Holding this little boy in my arms felt like coming home; I could feel my Charlie smiling.

Isaiah did very well on his ride to New Jersey, and he actually seemed to enjoy all the love he received from his transport angels. Everyone who saw him fought to see who could shower him with the most love. His true journey to healing had begun.

Isaiah remained in rescue for several months, during which time he gained weight, overcame seizures from malnourishment and imbalanced blood levels, revived his spirit, and developed a whopping "bigger than life" personality! Isaiah had finally become the healthy, happy dog that he was always meant to be, and it was time to find the perfect forever family for him.

That family came in the form of a thirty-something year old bachelor named Ray. Ray was an absolute hero of a man, who had a heart for special-needs dogs, particularly cockers. Ray had to say goodbye to two wonderful furkids, Barley and Dillon, each of whom had made a tremendous impact on his life, and he was ready to open his home and heart up to another one who needed him. Like many other adopters, Ray learned of Isaiah through Petfinder.com and contacted the rescue. Ray was a dream. Not only was he interested in adopting a dog who needed extra care, but he had an excellent vet reference and a fancy new sports car that Isaiah would look fabulous riding in!

It was clear to the rescue staff that Isaiah would be happy with Ray for his new dad. Animals always let us know if the match is right, and even though Isaiah hadn't shown a great fondness for men (and understandably so), he was immediately attached to the man who showed up to turn his life around.

Along with a new life, Ray also gave Isaiah a new name, which I didn't mind, because his new name was Job, a very fitting name for all that he had suffered through and survived.

I reunited with Job and met his wonderful dad, Ray, a few months ago, and I couldn't have been more thrilled to see the two of them together. Job was vibrant and healthy, and nosey like most cocker spaniels. He was everything that he deserved to be, and seemed oblivious to the pain of his past.

Ray was the proud father, beaming as he spoke of his boy, and keeping his eye on Job at all times. I think it was as much miracle for Ray as it was for Job, that the two had found one another.

A month later I entered Job in the Dogs Deserve Better calendar contest, and he won the cover page! This little one who had come from such misery and despair was now glowing on the cover of a national calendar, and representing all the other survivors who had come through to the heaven on the other side.

Sometimes life's just funny like that.

Six Dogs
Six Happy Endings

BY GAYLA FRANCES EVANS, DDB OHIO REP

ℬ

Bruno smiles, a happy boy after all he's been through

August first was quite the lucky day for six neglected Rotties, who were kept in filthy, deplorable conditions for years on end. They had no food or water bowls, so I don't know how they even drank; I do know a local Good Samaritan often provided them with water.

Three of the dogs were boarded up in a barn stall. Totally isolated, they could not get away from their own excrement or the overpoweringly-foul stench that emanated from their small enclosure. We had to trudge along five feet of disgusting muck, at least a foot deep, to free them from the living hell which they had endured for so long.

Another dog, Bruno, had his head stuck between two metal rods of cow fencing, and we have no idea how long he'd remained like this. His unfortunate companions, Della and Dyna, wanted out desperately, so my husband worked for fifteen minutes to remove the door to free them.

They were all skittish and fearful of humans at first, but eventually welcomed the leashes that would pull them to freedom.

One particular dog, Bud, was kept on a rope in a small living area, the floor of which was mostly covered with smelly, loose stool.

Ruger, his ears bleeding from fly strikes, was kept in the back stall behind Bud. Tyra was crammed in a cage which was kept in an upstairs room. It was much too small for her.

They all reeked horribly, had fleas, whipworms, hookworms, fly strikes and very long nails. Bud also had two tumors, double dewclaws, and a broken canine tooth.

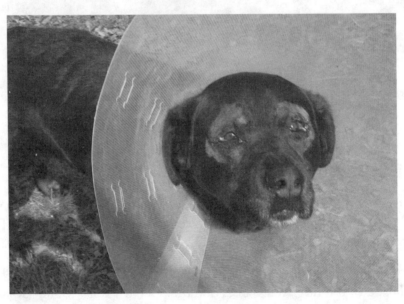

Bruno needed eye surgery. He had badly-inflamed eye infections due to turned-in lids—he could only squint because couldn't fully open his eyes. He has had Entropien surgery on both eyes now, and he looks good as new. He still has very bad hips, but is on medication.

Bruno has been in my care from day one; he's such a great dog who will moan with joy (and smile showing his pearly whites) when you love him up. He yearns to be touched and can't get enough attention.

Every day I see the thank you in Bruno's eyes for what we've done for him, and that's all I need to go on another day.

Dyna and Della, Ruger and Tyra, are all adopted and in new, loving homes. Theirs' is a truly much-deserved happy ending.

Bud is still with me as well. His tumors and dew-claws are now removed, the broken canine pulled, and now life seems good for Mr. Bud. A roly-poly fella', Bud eats and wiggles, content and thankful to be rescued.

Despite the ugliness these six dogs endured, they are all enjoying a new outlook on life these days—their ability to forget the bad and move on to the good is inspirational for all who meet them.

Banshee
The Rest of the Story

BY TAMIRA CI THAYNE, DOGS DESERVE BETTER FOUNDER

ℊ

Banshee looking at his mommy with eyes of love

I got the call early one weekday morning in August—a guy interested in Banshee. I'd had my fair share of people interested in adopting the 6-year-old purebred Black Labrador Retriever in the year since I'd rescued him, but come hell or high water I couldn't bring an adoption to close. I didn't hold my breath for this one either.

He'd seen Banshee's photo in the Altoona Mirror this past weekend, and wanted to hear more. He was in Coalport, Pennsylvania, about 5 miles from the spot I'd rescued the boy, and told me he lived on 20 acres and, yes, there was a pond.

My ears perked up. One of the reasons Banshee's had a hard time finding a home is that I've been kinda picky about who he goes to live

128

with. But not really—I mean, I know the dog's needs, and the dog needs a lot more than your average couch potato dog. He needs room to run, he needs a place to swim, and he needs someone to throw a ball for him.

Preferably, into the water.

Plus, he needs someone to devote himself to. A person really should be worthy of this devotion, no?

Banshee is a one-human dog, more than any other I've met, and—as it turns out—for now I'm that human. It makes for some big responsibility.

It also makes for a teensy bit of reciprocal adoration and therefore a reluctance to part ways with him. I rarely admit this even to myself, and...well...now to you. (Don't tell anyone.) I mean, how can you witness this dog staring at you lovingly day in and day out for 14 months and not begin to feel a smidgen of passion in return for the beast?

He's a wily little coyote-dog!

Home in Altoona, complete with swimming pool? Pool, sweet, BUT—no fenced yard, crowded city life, and no room to run. Plus, she sounds like a smoker. Nuh-uh.

Home with two small kids and another Lab who swims? Maybe on the Lab, but the small kids, no way. They'd be plowed over repeatedly until someone got hurt and someone else had to go. That someone else would inevitably be Banshee.

We don't call him "The Freight Train" for nothin'.

If Banshee wants to go somewhere, say, like with you in the van, and you are between him and say, the door, watch out. You are about to be shoved unceremoniously into the lamp while a big black block-head of a dog pushes past you and rushes to the back of the vehicle, circling and spinning, waiting to get in.

Admittedly, dog-trainer failure that I am, I know that he should be better-schooled than this by now. He should be sitting patiently back from the door, intently measuring my facial expressions and de-meanor, and accepting his fate with grace if it's a day he has to stay.

But that is wishful thinking. If I'm truly paying attention, I can put him into a sit and, if I maintain eye contact, keep him from rushing the door, but truth be told most of the time I'm focused only on whatever *I'm* rushing out the door for, and not on what Banshee is up to or where he is at this particular moment.

I find myself tricking him back into the house at least once a day. It works because as long as he thinks that's where I'm going, he's up for it too. When he does get to ride along with me, he's the best-behaved van-dog in the world. He's just content to be there—with the woman he adores—laying on the blanket behind the barrier, watching and sleeping, in a state of total relaxation.

Banshee's one of those dogs that really needs a job, hopefully one that pays well so he can start chipping in for the bills around here. He became the impetus for and focus of my first book, *Scream Like Banshee: 29 Days of Tips and Tales to Keep your Sanity as a Doggie Foster Parent*, because shortly after his rescue he slipped into some severe separation anxiety, and it almost got him killed.

The cliffhanger of *Scream Like Banshee*—totally blown now—is whether Banshee survives his suicide-attempt; but since you're here reading *The Rest of the Story*, it's safe to assume he does. (Spoiler Alert.) I'm keeping secrets about HOW he almost does himself in, though, so if you're curious you'll have to just run along and read it for yourself.

I first saw Banshee's black form chained to a doghouse about three years previous to obtaining his freedom. He was housed beside the driveway, to the left of a nicer-than-average home, just past Sir Barney's Restaurant on the way to Prince Gallitzin State Park in Flinton, Pennsylvania.

I clucked my tongue in disgust, like I always do, gave my pitying "Oooooh, look at that poor dog," and started my normal bitch about what is wrong with people. This became my pattern each time I passed by, straining my neck to see if he was still there, and launching into my tirade as I again ascertained that he indeed remained. We put doorhangers on their mailbox more than once, "Dogs Deserve Better than Life on a Chain" signs by both stop signs, but yet there he stayed, forgotten, on his chain.

Banshee ended up coming to me for rescue in a round-about way, through the vet that we use to spay/neuter our freed doggies. His caretaker was growing senile, and becoming increasingly obsessed with Banshee's welfare. His son called our vet to find out if anyone would be interested in a Black Lab, and when the vet tech found out that he was living chained, gave him our number and told him we'd find placement for the dog.

When I spoke to the son, telling him I would come to meet the dog, get photos and a description, and find him a Lab rescue or foster home, he was decidedly reluctant to bring me to where the dog lived.

It was all I could do to suppress a smile and pretend to know nothing about the doorhangers and signs when he revealed the location to me . . . apparently our efforts HAD gotten under the guardian's skin after all!

Banshee would win because of my persistence.

When I met Banshee for the first time face to face, I was surprised to see that he was wearing a harness instead of a collar, and a lightweight tether instead of a chain. I was inclined to look upon his guardian more favorably for a bit (and I did pity him because he reminded me of my grandfather), until I saw that Banshee bore scars under his neck, probably from an embedded collar. He also growled if you touched his neck. I asked the son if his collar had embedded, and he admitted that it had and he supposed that was indeed why he was now wearing a harness instead of a collar.

So much for giving the caretaker a break!

We placed Banshee with a Lab rescue in southeastern Pennsylvania where he was neutered and had a tumor removed from his wrist. He was boarded in a vet's office kennel instead of a foster home, and he ended up getting kicked out of the rescue because he kept growling at people at the vet's office. I guess the lecture I gave him about minding his P's and Q's went right over his head!

Back to me he came. I really didn't have room for one more at the time, and I wasn't inclined to bring a growling male into my home, but since I'd been the one to commit to taking him off that chain, I knew it was on me to house him as a temporary measure and continue to look for an adequate foster home or Lab rescue.

We know how that turned out. Here it was 14 months later, and Banshee was still with me, and still seeking his forever home and family. His fur has grown sleek and shiny, and he spends a fair amount of time running in the woods with his pack, fetching balls from the stream, and following me around everywhere I go.

He has a pretty good life.

If he's to go to another home, it has to be better than this one, or I see no point to it. He needs to have daily access to water for swimming, room to run and play fetch, and someone who loves and values him for what he is: a crazy, constantly moving, sweet but annoying, funny, gem of a Lab.

I asked the caller what he's looking for in a dog, and he told me he was thinking of getting a doghouse and putting Banshee out back on a chain. I said, "Come again? Do you know what Dogs Deserve Better does? This dog came from a chain, and there's no way he's going back."

The caller got really quiet for a minute, and then he said, "I'm sorry, I was just telling you what I thought you wanted to hear. Here's the thing, I can't adopt Banshee, and I don't believe in letting your dog outside on a chain either. I do live on 20 acres, but I rent and I already have one dog. The property owner won't let me have another.

"I just needed to make sure Banshee is ok and isn't going to be put down. I know exactly where he lived, 'cause I saved his life one day. I just had to call and find out."

Now I was confused. "What do you mean you saved his life?" I asked.

"My wife and I were driving by his house, and I saw that something was funny with his neck. I stopped the car and went to look at him, and I saw that his neck was damn near sawed in half by his collar!

"I was furious. I went and got the owner and started screaming at him to get the dog help and get it now. I couldn't believe he didn't even notice that his dog was like that! I made sure he put that dog in the car and started heading to the vet's before I would even leave.

"I've noticed for quite awhile he wasn't there anymore, and the doghouse is gone too, but I didn't know where he was or what had happened to him. Please tell me you won't put him down, because I'll find some way to get him out of there if you are."

I reassured him that Banshee had already been here for over a year, we'd spent a ton of money to save his life during the separation anxiety phase, and I had no intention of putting him down now. I also told him he was more than welcome to come by and visit him anytime, and about the book bearing Banshee's name.

He was so relieved! He thanked me sincerely for giving Banshee a chance, and I thanked him for having the courage to confront Banshee's guardian and force him to treat his neck before it was too late. Not many people, especially men, have the courage to get involved.

I'm thinking Banshee's down two lives so far, but isn't it only cats who have nine lives? Banshee must have himself a guardian angel or two making sure he has time to be a dog and know the love that every dog deserves.

And someday, a home that is worthy of my boy will come along, and he can have the life of his dreams—running on that farm, ball in his mouth, and a daily swim with a loving caretaker.

Or, he'll stay here with his runner-up mommy and settle for a pretty damn good life that's still 1,000 miles ahead of his last one. We'll see.

Hitting the
Ground Running

BY TIM TREYBAL, DDB MINNESOTA REP

❧

Doc, now a happy, happy boy

I had only just been approved as a Dog Deserve Better representative and still hadn't learned the ropes when Doc's neighbor contacted me. I was told about a 24/7-penned Black Lab who had spent six years of his life in a small, chain-link-fenced area. He was allowed shelter in a stuffy storage room with little to no ventilation. The outside area was riddled with foot-high weeds and the inside room was a defecation nightmare. This was in Minnesota, so the temperature extreme for a 24/7 outside dog was significant.

After sending out a brochure and awareness letter to the dog's guardians, I received a call from the lady of the house offering to surrender her dog. She swore she'd done well by the dog, but believed he could have a better life. She said I could have him in two weeks. I was given no explanation why I would have to wait two weeks before rescuing him.

We both live in a small rural community where everyone knows everyone's business, and secrets are rarely hidden. It happened a mere two days later that the truth was revealed in the police report section of the local newspaper. The article stated the dog's guardian had been fined for allowing her dog to "run at large." This was only the frosty Minnesota icing on the cake.

The article continued to disclose that the dog had been quarantined for ten days after biting a person walking by the home. Basically, the Lab had escaped his prison-pen and bitten a passerby, the *real* reason his guardian decided to surrender him to me. This also explained why I was asked to wait two weeks before I picked him up. The dog, not updated on required rabies shots, was in quarantine. I ran to my bathroom mirror expecting to see the word "Sucker" tattooed on my forehead.

The dog's name was Liberty (ironic, I know), but for his new life he needed a new name, so I renamed him Doc after my grandpa. Few people knew my grandpa's real name, and he was known by most only by his nickname, Doc.

I knew right away the cause of the bite stemmed from the isolated dog finally getting loose. His excitement was brought on by a tense situation and the dog lashed out from pent up frustration. I couldn't blame a dog for not being socialized and trained, but I cold give the same dog a second chance to prove himself.

I called the vet holding him in quarantine, explaining his guardian agreed to surrender the dog to me. He said, "Tim, you don't want this dog, he's just plain mean." This reinforced my experience with many vets and vet techs—they may know how to treat physical problems, but know little about dog behavior. I didn't back down and Doc was surrendered to me only ten days after the unfortunate incident.

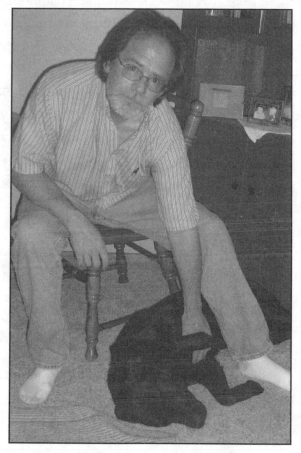

Tim, rubbing a relaxed Doc's belly

On the night of the surrender, his guardian did everything she could to convince me Liberty had the best life and a clean environment to live in. She had ten days to make the place as immaculate as she could before I would pay her a visit—it wasn't enough time for her to hide foot high weeds and a urine stench in the storeroom that would gag most people and even their dogs.

I got him up to date on vaccines, and heartworm and fecal tested. He was wormed, neutered, and the treated for fleas with Capstar and Promeris. He had an inflamed open sore on his scrotum, which the vet attributed to laying on the urine filled carpet he slept on.

Doc resides in my home now. He is relishing the life a dog should have. I have three dogs myself, who have taken him under their wing with open paws. He's a medium-energy dog, with only a few issues; he goes for pack walks, where he's learning to walk beside me and relax on the leash.

He has now learned commands such as "sit" and "down," but prefers to just roll over for a chest and tummy scratch. He's such a character! Doc loves to play bow and when he runs it's with the enthusiasm of playtime. He's a happy boy living the happy dog dream!

Yep, both of us hit the ground running. Doc hit the ground running with the zest to have fun after his nightmare stint of living penned and isolated. I hit the ground running as a Dogs Deserve Better representative with the passion to breathe new life into backyard dogs, preparing them to become cherished family members, as they deserve.

Kids Who Care:
Love Overcomes Selfishness

BY CHERIE SMITH, DDB PENNSYLVANIA ADOPTER

℘

Justin and Sweet Pea hang out at home

My son Justin has become a dog advocate for chained/neglected dogs and has been trying to spread the word about bringing dogs into homes so they can be loved as a pet. His journey began one October while attending an event for dogs called Woofstock in Harrisburg, Pennsylvania. There he met Sweet Pea, a dog who was chained in Georgia and was being fostered by Dogs Deserve Better. I believe that it was love at first sight the minute their eyes met and of course, I thought she was just the sweetest. We completed the adoption application, went through a home visit, and once we were accepted, Justin and Craig (his step-dad) drove to State College to meet Tami, her foster mom, and Sweet Pea.

Sweet Pea had been adopted by a family who no longer wanted the responsibility for her and asked Tami to take her back. Once Tami had her back in her care, she noticed that Sweet Pea was not her happy-go-lucky self anymore, and knew that something must have happened to her in the former home. While this angered her, she had no proof, so there wasn't much she could do except give Sweet Pea the love and acceptance she'd been missing.

We were aware of this when we met Sweet Pea and wanted to give her the best life possible. Once home, Justin showered her with toys and treats but she just didn't understand what she was supposed to do with them. After a year, she has come out of her shell and just LOVES her treats and toys. When she runs with Lacy, her sister dog, she actually bounces and prances—it's the cutest thing!

Justin's biological father has never had much compassion for animals or people. During Justin's journey with Sweet Pea and volunteering with Dogs Deserve Better and Angels Among Us (as well as sponsoring and donating toys, treats, and dog beds to these organizations), he has attempted to inform his dad of the good things he is doing and hoping that his father will tell him "good job Justin" or "I am so proud of you." Unfortunately, these words have never come out of his mouth. He usually just changes the subject so that he doesn't have to say anything about Justin's efforts.

Recently they were speaking on the phone and a comment was made by his father that he believes dogs belong outside, not inside the home with the family.

With shock and disbelief in his voice, Justin said, "What?" His father repeated himself. He then proceeded to tell Justin that the only type of dog that should be allowed inside are dogs like Cocker Spaniels because they are small.

He also told Justin, "Why would you want a dog in the house? That's like having a horse living with you; plus, they bark when you are trying to have a conversation as well as during the night when you are trying to sleep. I'm sure you know what I mean, buddy, since you have two dogs."

Justin, very calmly, replied, "Dogs do not deserve to be left outside because they want to be part of your family. If you keep them outside, why have a dog at all? Our dogs do not bark in the middle of the night, because they are inside sleeping with us, their pack. They only bark if and when necessary."

Of course, his father said nothing. As a mother, I couldn't have been prouder of Justin but at the same time, I felt the pain of knowing that Justin realized all the conversations they had had over the past year were for nothing.

His father will never understand what he is trying to do for dogs nor does he really care. Justin will not get the praise or validation from his father that he has wanted to hear for many, many years.

This will not deter Justin from spreading the word because he truly is on a mission. Not only is Justin trying to free dogs from their chains, but in a way, he is trying to free himself from the emotional chains of his father.

Justin is learning to be compassionate even though his father is not. He is learning to give because his father does not, and he is learning to become his own person so that one day he can pass down a more empathetic legacy to his own children and family.

Justin working a DDB Booth at Woofstock

She May Be Nuttin' but a Hound Dog, But She's A Good Friend Of Mine

BY BELEN BRISCO, DDB FLORIDA REP

❧

Dakota is what I call "a good 'ol hound mix." I first met her on July 2 in North Naples, Florida. She was not only chained outside, but she wore a harness around her body because a chain alone wouldn't hold her. Imagine that? She was still just a pup, barely a year old, and a chain around her neck couldn't keep her confined.

She lived on a farm, far away from the house being built on the property. She was close enough to see the comings and goings of her caretakers, but too far away to interact with them. Her days and nights were spent alone. The bucket to hold her water was filthy. She was supplied with a doghouse, but I imagined this would provide little, if any, relief from the heat of a Florida summer.

Instinct taught Dakota it was cooler underground. She did what most dogs do, dug a hole deep into the dirt to stay as cool as possible. The steady swarm of Florida insects had their way with her as she was not able to escape them. This was Dakota's life, though not an existence any human or animal would choose voluntarily, especially not a pack animal like a dog. What could she do? It was the hand she was dealt, her fate was sealed. Or was, I should say, until the day I opened my email and read the subject line, "A farm dog needs help."

I received an email about a dog chained in Naples, Florida, but the problem was the sender failed to provide me with an address. I hadn't the faintest idea where the dog could be found in all of Naples. The only person who knew my email contact was out of town. I called and left messages, then patiently waited.

My call was finally returned on July 2, when I was given a general idea where the dog was located. It was farm country and I was given a local's version of directions, you know the kind: "You can't miss it! You just pass the school house on the left, go by the big tree, then you're gonna want to turn right, but don't 'cause ya really don't want to go that way, you'll just think ya do…"

Not knowing what kind of situation I was walking into I called the area's animal control and explained what I was up to. I was assured the animal control had my back and was told not to put myself in harm's way, just drive by to get the address. Ok, we'll see!

My informant said Dakota's guardian had gone back and forth on the issue of re-homing her. Just in case, I proceeded with necessary arrangements if the dog should happen to be surrendered to me. I called my good friend Karin, also a DDB volunteer, to assist me. Like any good minuteman or animal rescuer, she was ready. My daughter Leah, with camera in hand, completed our brave trio.

We loaded food, water, and a crate in the back of our vehicle. We were equipped if the trip should happen to end with a successful rescue. My friend and DDB volunteer Karen with an "E," not to be confused with Karin with an "I," said she'd foster if need be.

It took an hour and fifteen minutes to locate the spot where we were told we'd find the dog. As we rolled up the driveway toward the house, we saw her. She was looking at us, excitedly jumping up and down as if to say "Over here, here I am!"

"Yes, we see you Dakota!" I thought. "Now," I wondered, "is there anyone else here for us to see? Is anyone home?" The house was in the process of being built, and there was one truck parked in the driveway. I didn't see anyone around, but I intended to take a closer look. We all evacuated the vehicle and began casing the joint. Karin and I looked around for human life, while Leah began taking photos of Dakota. I guess that may have been why we weren't so quick to notice when someone came out of the house.

He was an older gentleman with a heavy southern accent. It's comical how all of the sudden my Texas drawl came back to me when I heard him speak. I always want to be polite so I began with, "Hello Sir. How are you? Is this your dawg?" Ok, maybe too much Southern charm, I was laying it on a little thick.

The gentleman explained that the dog belonged to his granddaughter. How many times have we heard that? No one wants to claim a dog as his when the dog isn't properly cared for. In this case, it may have been true, who knows. Supposedly his granddaughter asked her granddad to keep her dog, because well... she couldn't! I forget the long line of excuses that came spilling out after that.

"Well, then, is it ok if I take the dog?" I asked. "We can give her a nice place to live, have her vetted to make sure she is healthy and all."

His answer was disappointing. "Naw, my granddaughter would be upset."

I have to tell you, I kinda' liked this guy. He was very mannerly; he honestly seemed to be caught up in a bad situation with his grand-daughter and her dog. He wanted to be nice and help his grand-daughter, but it ended with him not feeling too great about the pup's current circumstances.

His first response was no, I couldn't take the dog. When it comes to doing the right thing, however, the word no doesn't stop me from trying to change someone's mind.

I kept right along chitchatting with him, telling him about some of the ordinances he was already breaking and so on. During our conversation, Leah was still taking photos and Karin was trying to play with Dakota. Dakota was jumping for joy at her company and the attention she was receiving.

My thoughts began to wander toward my entourage's antics with the pup, when I heard a word that shook me back to the conversation. He mentioned something about coyotes. "Coyotes?" I blurted out. "What happens if this poor pup is eaten by coyotes while you're gone?"

He then looked at me, and with a sideways glance he said, "Take the pup."

"Good call!" I thought to myself. I couldn't image how he would have felt had he come home one day to find poor Ms. Dakota injured or worse. It could happen easily enough, chained to a stationary ob-ject without a way for her to escape or defend herself. It would be harder to explain to his granddaughter that coyotes got her dog, than telling her he gave the dog to someone who would find her a good home.

Karin didn't have any luck getting the harness off. It was jury-rigged in such a way only pliers could free Dakota from her chains. Luckily, the man with the thick Southern accent had a pair on hand. After applying a little elbow grease, she was free! The release form for Dakota was signed and witnessed and then the courteous gentlemen offered me a tour of his new home. "Well, heck yeah!"

It was the least I could do and I appreciated his Southern hospitality. I spent about ten minutes viewing the home he was building for his wife. After spending time with him and educating him on the dangers of dog chaining, I could see he was truly happy for Dakota to have a chance at a better life.

Dakota was coming home with us that very day! The next few minutes in the car was spent with Karin and Leah sending text messages to inform everyone that Dakota was off the chain. By the time we reached his new foster home, Karen was already standing by to receive her new guest.

Dakota was vetted the next morning. She was tested and found to be heartworm negative, but she had hookworms, fleas, an ear infection, and few a hot spots. We left the vet's office and went to see our good friends at "Island Paws" for a nice long bath.

The trip home was quiet. Dakota was peaceful; she seemed secure, as if she knew her life would only get better from this point on. Like a baby with a full tummy, Dakota was ready for a nap. As I drove her back to Karen's I looked at her with thankfulness in my heart for the great team of animal lovers I have to rely on. Dakota felt safe, relaxed and her eyes said to me, "Thank you for a great day!"

"No," I said, "Thank YOU, Dakota, for giving me purpose."

Several days later, Karen, the foster and DDB volunteer, emailed to say she had fallen in love with Dakota. She wanted Dakota's foster home to become her forever home. She asked if Dakota might stay permanently to live amongst the rest of her pack. It was a lucky day for Dakota. She hit the jackpot!

A single rescue of a little 'ol hound dog sure enlisted the help of a lot of people. Dakota's rescue was made possible by the originator of the email, "A Farm Dog Needs Help," Terri in Naples for leading us there; special people like Karin, Karen, and Leah; my veterinarian and the groomers at Island Paws for fitting Dakota into their schedules on short notice; and last, but certainly not least, the Dogs Deserve Better volunteers, donors, and members who believe and support the freeing of dogs. I send out my heartfelt thanks to all of you.

Cinder-Ella
Finds Her Prince

BY TAMMI KINMAN RUPPERT, DDB KENTUCKY REP

ॐ

Ella just after rescue, so, so skinny

I became a Dogs Deserve Better representative a little more a year ago. I recently went back through my successful rescues, and was surprised to learn I've been able to rescue 25 dogs in the course of a year! What's most amazing is that each dog's life went from a horrible day-to-day existence to any dog's dream life. I have to admit, being a DDB rep is the most rewarding, but toughest job I've ever held, especially since I don't get paid—with money that is. The rewarding experience of watching a dog going from misery to happiness—and knowing I'm the one making it happen—could never compare to monetary gain.

In May of this year I went to a small, out of the way rural shelter to pick up a dog for a Golden Retriever rescue group for whom I do transports. It was at this shelter that I met Sally, later to become Ella.

If you aren't familiar with animal rescue transports, individuals volunteer their time and using their own vehicles, take dogs and cats from point A to point B to meet the next leg of the transport. Transport information is posted in run sheets, mapped out with times, scheduled stops, information about the animals, and the necessary contact information for each driver, as well as the sending and receiving rescues.

The shelter where I was picking up the Retriever was by far the worst I have ever stepped foot in. It was in the middle of nowhere, on a country road by the county landfill and a rendering plant. Almost every dog at the shelter would be put down; it was not a public-friendly place. Since I was there anyway, I looked around, checked out the establishment, and took a peak at the unfortunate dogs held there.

Stuck in an out-of-the-way concrete kennel, away from all the other dogs, sat the saddest looking, hunched-over, emaciated German Shepherd I've ever laid eyes on. My heart broke just to look at her. I asked the animal control officer permission to take her for a walk. He said yes, and off we went.

She was filthy, skinny, and covered in ticks. All she wanted was to lean into me for affection. When we returned I asked her story and was told she was a court case, seized from her guardians who beat her with a garden hose while she was chained up.

That was all I needed to hear. I had to get her out of there. The ACO explained she had to stay at the shelter for at least 10 days. I told him I would be working on finding a home for her during that time. I sadly left her behind. I'm filled with regret when I'm forced to walk away from a shelter; leaving behind so many animals, knowing I don't have the resources to save them all. When an especially needy dog touches my soul, I can't walk away without feeling haunted by the dog's image. This was my emotional state as I left Ella that day.

I had recently rescued another German Shepherd named Shiloh. I had several people interested in adopting her, so I hoped someone would be willing to adopt a skinny, abused, sweet young German Shepherd in desperate need of a good home.

I contacted a young man I knew, whose family had at one time bred German Shepherds, but now they remained family members. They had recently lost one of their pack, and they were looking for another as company for their grieving male, Lupo. They embraced the idea of rescuing a female in need of a loving home.

I described Ella's poor condition and abusive past. They decided she was the dog for them; they wanted to provide a happy life for her, sight unseen. The family lived about four hours north of Cincinnati, so we arranged to meet halfway in Columbus, Ohio. I went back and picked up Sally as soon as the shelter allowed her release. I brought her to my home for a couple of days to watch her enjoy her life off the chain and outside of the shelter's cage. I smiled every single time I glanced her way, and I especially enjoyed feeding her as many treats as she wanted!

Ella and Lupo wrestle and play in the living room

I explained to her on the drive to Columbus that this was the first day of the rest of her life. Her new Dad, Justin, was very excited; he told me they were looking forward to turning Sally into the dog she was meant to be.

Their home was perfect for her! It was love at first sight for Sally and Justin and this is when he decided to name her Ella, after Ella Fitzgerald. Justin is a gifted musician and thought the name fitting; for me, her name reminds me of a shorter version of Cinderella, as her story is complete with a fairytale ending.

Ella has blossomed into a beautiful dog. She lives happily ever after in her own family's castle. She finally knows what being loved is as she lives her enchanted existence with her very own Prince Justin.

I feel like a fairy godmother, waving my magic wand to end Ella's charmed story with a "Bibbity, Bobbity, Boo!"

One Luckie Girl
Her Name Might Have Saved Her

BY PAM CHEATHAM, DDB GEORGIA REP

⅋

A plea came over the rescue network for a "bonded pair" of dogs: Gretchen, a German Shepherd and Buddy, a Black Labrador Retriever. I'm including them in Luckie's story because without Gretchen and Buddy, Luckie's story wouldn't have turned out so lucky.

While Ginger was at the shelter in Walker County pulling Gretchen and Buddy, she noticed another dog, a very petite German Shepherd female who looked like she was starving. A shelter worker told Ginger that this tiny Shepherd had been found dragging a chain and was very young. They named her Luckie but they decided not to post her on the network for adoption or rescue. Her time was up.

As an afterthought, Ginger took her, too.

Wow, the name worked!

When Molly told me that I'd be picking up an extra dog from Ginger, I thought "I'll figure something out."

Now I had to drive home with Luckie. I installed her in a spare room in our basement. Turns out my husband didn't notice her; from a distance, he thought I was walking one of our Shepherds. For the next two days, I took Luckie everywhere I went. She drove with me to work on a fencing project, she went with me to run errands and to check on other dogs. So far, her name was working.

Luckie went to US Canine boot camp to learn how to relate to other dogs. By the time Luckie was finished with all her medical needs and ready for her "close-up," my husband had gotten used to the idea of another foster and he took some beautiful pictures.

The real proof of the power of her name came when Moira saw Luckie's posting and contacted us from Jacksonville, Florida. This family was the perfect match for Luckie. Moira was an attorney, married to a Naval submarine commander, with super-achieving children Ayla and Liam. They had lost their beloved Malamute of 11 years the summer before to an incurable degenerative disease. While they knew that no dog could replace Aquila, they deeply missed the companionship a dog brings to the family. As a family, they enjoyed running, hiking and other activities, and were looking for a dog who would be able to participate fully. How could Luckie get so lucky?

By this time I had been Luckie's mom for nearly four months. To say we loved each other is an understatement. We'd driven all over the state, thousands of miles together. We walked and ran two and three times every day, rain, shine, dark, light. We practiced and trained and could read each other's minds.

On the day of her adoption, we drove to a McDonald's halfway between Atlanta and Jacksonville, to meet Bill, Luckie's new dad. I was walking Luckie on leash when Bill drove up.

He opened the hatchback; she took one look at him and jumped right up into his car and laid down. She looked at me to say thanks and was ready to go home with Bill.

Over the next few weeks, every email brought more pictures and stories of Luckie and her new family. She had her first swim in the pond, her first trip to the dog park, her first beach vacation, her first trip to visit the grandparents, etc.

There was a little bump in the road when she started lunging at other dogs on leash. Moira didn't lose her cool, but contacted professional trainers, and worked with Luckie and the family to get her back on track. At Christmas, Luckie joined the rest of the family on the family Christmas card. The following year Ayla wrote an essay about Luckie for school, describing how Luckie has taught her so much.

Luckie and her family moved to Virginia this summer. She has new parks to explore and new routines to master. She also has her family, her pack, who she loves with all her heart.

An Old
Dog's Value

BY JOE MARINGO, DIRECTOR, SOUTHWEST PENNSYLVANIA RETRIEVER

RESCUE ORGANIZATION (S.P.A.R.R.O.)

&

Zena lifts her nose to the sun

It was a bitter cold January day, just like most January days at the Hillside SPCA in Pottsville, Pennsylvania. The temperature was hovering right at zero in mid afternoon. Even so, cars and people were coming and going. Dogs were barking and playing in the snow. Staff and volunteers were attending to the chores of the day. Little did anyone know that two things would happen on this frigid afternoon that would change the lives of several people and one very special dog.

First, a news crew from WNEP-16 in Scranton arrived to do a

story on the frigid temps and the many area dogs who were forced to spend their days and nights chained outside.

Second, as the crew was setting up in the adoptions office of the shelter to start their interview, a car pulled into the lot and a well-dressed man came over to Liz, one of the humane agents there. "I'm here for my appointment," he told her.

Puzzled, her reply was "What do you have an appointment for?" She hoped maybe he had come to adopt a new companion or find out how the adoption process worked.

Sadly, that was not the case at all. "I have an appointment to have my dog put to sleep."

This really confused Liz, since Hillside is a No-Kill facility. "I'm sorry, but we don't euthanize animals here, we're a No-Kill shelter."

It turned out the man and his family had made an appointment with another shelter some distance away, but had driven here by mistake. "Well, can you just put her to sleep for me?"

Again, Liz told him, "As I said, we don't euthanize dogs. If you want that done you will have to drive to the shelter you have the appointment with."

"Well I'm very busy and don't have time to drive all the way across the county, and besides I've missed my appointment now. Can I just leave her here with you?"

"If you would like to sign her over, we will take her in and try to find her a new home."

"Well, I don't know who would want a seventeen-year-old dog, but you can take her. Where do I sign?"

Liz had him fill out the surrender form and went with him to get the dog out of the car. When he opened the door one of the saddest old dogs Liz had ever seen literally fell to the ground at her feet. She looked at the form the man had filled out for some info on the dog.

Her name was Zena, she was seventeen years old and had spent her entire life on a chain. While the man, his wife and kids drove away in their warm, comfortable car, Liz gathered the old arthritic dog up and helped her toward the office.

The news crew had just gotten their equipment set up and turned on the camera to check the settings when a sobbing Liz came through the door. It was fate, or a divine hand that told the cameraman to keep filming.

"He just opened the door and she fell out at my feet," Liz sobbed loudly. The other staff jumped to action, wrapping Zena in blankets trying to warm her up. "She has been chained out for 17 years. This is probably the first time in months she has been warm!" That was the lead in to the story about bitter cold temps and dogs forced to live outside on the six o'clock news in Scranton that night. It was also my introduction to the Hillside SPCA and to the heroin of this story.

My friend Julie always sends me interesting pictures, stories and internet links. She is particularly fond of the Hillside shelter. When she saw the story online later that night, she just naturally sent it on to me. Not knowing what to expect I clicked on the "WATCH VIDEO" link. The first thing I saw was the staggering old black dog with the white muzzle, and Liz sobbing and telling her story. I was only ten seconds into a two minute video and I was crying right along with them.

Next, I saw them in the office offering her a bowl of food. The dog seemed confused, and it was then that I noticed the dog did not seem to have any eyes. It looked like she just had two empty sockets. The video went on to talk about other dogs and cats living outside in the freezing cold, but all I could see was the old black dog. The odd thing I remembered was the sheer look of joy on her face at just the slightest attention people were giving her. A warm blanket and a kind touch made her face light up with pleasure. I emailed Julie right away to let her know that she had once again brought this big tough guy to tears.

There was no sleeping that entire night. The anguish that Liz felt for the plight of this gentle soul, and her smiling white face filled my mind the entire night. At 8 a.m., another email to Julie, "I'm calling Hillside when they open. If she is still there, I'm adopting that black dog!"

The shelter website said they opened at eleven that day, so at 11:01 a.m. I was on the phone. I had met their other Humane Agent, Janine, once about a year earlier. Janine was on the video as well, so that is who I asked for when someone answered the phone. A few seconds later Janine was on the line. It is much easier talking to someone you know, even if it was just a brief meeting, so I was happy to hear her voice.

"Hi Janine, this is Joe from Southwest Pennsylvania Retriever Rescue, do you remember me?"

"Well sure, how are you doing?"

"I'm doing great, but I have a question for you. Do you still have that old black dog that was on the news video last night?"

"Yes we do, why?"

"Is anyone interested in her? I assume you have had a few calls with the publicity that story got last night."

"No, not a single call. You're the only person who has even asked about her."

This absolutely broke my heart. How could others not have been moved by what they had seen, as I was? Had the world become so callous as to not even care about an old dog?

"Well Janine, would you like to place her in a happy forever home?"

"ARE YOU SERIOUS! Are you considering her?"

You could hear the excitement and thrill in her voice, along with just the slightest hint of pleading. "It would be my honor to let her live out the rest of her life here with me and my family."

The rest of the call was a bit frantic. There was a thud and I could here Janine yelling in the background "SOMEONE WANTS HER, SOMEONE WANTS TO ADOPT ZENA!" Janine put Liz on the phone and I got all the important info about Zena. She was seventeen years old, had spent all or most of her life on a chain outside, she was very stiff with arthritis and had a hard time walking. She was also totally blind and probably deaf as well.

Now to most people these health problems might have caused them to have second thoughts about adopting Zena, but not me. I did not hear one thing that gave me any reason to question my intentions. My mind just kept going back to her smile, as long as she had that everything else was minor. Liz and I talked for a few more minutes and I told her I would make the 600-mile round trip three days later.

I spent the next three days just like a proud parent, sending pictures and the video link to all my friends. I also posted her pictures and info on the three Labrador chat forums of which I'm a member. The response was as I expected, hundreds of people and friends sending best wishes for Zena and their thanks for saving her. A few people even said they where moved to tears and that they where going to try to help dogs or shelters in their own area.

Tuesday morning dawned sunny and clear for the first time in days. The thought of driving to the Pocono's with the potential for bad weather was the one thing that could have thrown a wrench into the plans. I warmed up the truck, loaded up my best buddy Blacky the Labrador and headed east. The trip was pretty routine. As always, Blacky, who is my heart-dog and constant companion, lay quietly on his bed in the front seat, his head on my lap. Halfway there I had a flash of inspiration. I called WNEP-16 in Scranton to see if they were interested in doing a follow up on the original story. The lady I spoke to said they might be able to get a camera out, but since the new president was being sworn into office today, the news crews were pretty busy. Someone would call and let me know if they could make it or not. The call never came.

About 1 p.m., I pulled up the steep road to the shelter. The lot was filled with cars and some were even parked along the road. I managed to squeeze into a spot next to the cat building, which was good since I had also brought a large donation of cat food for the shelter. When I got out of my truck I was surprised to see an SUV from WNEP-16 there. They had gotten the cameraman from the first story to come down and film the happy ending. We shook hands and made our introductions, then with cameraman in tow, I set off to find Janine.

"Hi Joe, how was the trip?"

"Long, but worth every minute and mile."

"Would you like to meet your girl?"

"I sure would! I'll follow you," and off we went. We entered a small office and there lying on a dog bed in the corner was Zena. People have asked me what I thought when I first saw her, and my reply was "She's dirty, smells bad, her hair is falling out in clumps, she's blind, deaf, arthritic and without a doubt the most beautiful girl in the world!"

Of course, it didn't matter to me how she looked or smelled, just that her smile was still there. I bent down to pet her, forgetting that she was blind and deaf, and my touch startled her, but just for a moment. She quickly realized I was there to pet her and sat up, leaning firmly into me. Before I knew it, she was ROO-ROOING in delight while the camera caught it all on tape. After a few moments, she stood up and started walking in circles around me. This greatly surprised the staff as they had hardly seen her walk in the days since she had arrived. Then the real surprise. She walked over, licked my face, let out a small bark, sat down and offered me her paw. It caught me off guard and I didn't have a chance to receive it before she had to put it back on the ground to steady herself. They filmed a bit longer and then we went outside for a short interview.

Zena walked down the hill to my truck to meet Blacky. Blacky is a very good boy, and while he is afraid of most people, he never met a dog he did not love. We had a few pictures taken of me, Zena and

Blacky, then it was time to head for home. I thanked the cameraman for doing the original story with Zena in it, and Janine for taking Zena in and allowing me to adopt her.

The ride home found me answering my cell phone every few minutes. Everyone wanted to know if I had her and if she was as sweet as she seemed on the video. My answer was, "She is even SWEETER!"

Once we arrived home I offered her some food, water, threw another log in the fireplace, and set out several dog beds for her. I didn't know if it would be too warm for her thick fur, so I had beds all over the family room for her. Again she surprised me by picking the one only three feet from the fireplace and falling quickly asleep. The next morning, eight hours later, she was in the exact same place. Zena was finally home.

After one week, Zena was fitting in like she had lived here for years. The other dogs all loved her, and my wife Barb loved her too. Zena's contagious smile has moved to my face now. Every time I pet her, or walk her, or even just look at her, I find myself grinning from ear to ear. Perma-smile is what they call it I think. Each day she is a little bit stronger, a little more steady on her feet.

We have found that she can hear, at least a little bit. She will come if I whistle, and she can without doubt hear the sound of kibble falling into a stainless food bowl. She barks if she needs out to potty, and she has a pretty good memory of the family room and front yard. Unfortunately, there will be no happy news about her eyes, as they are beyond repair. Our wonderful vet, Dr. Bowser (yes, what better name for a vet!) says it was probably Glaucoma that was left untreated and the pressure caused the eyes to rupture and atrophy. No matter though, because blind dogs see with their hearts! That is so true, because whatever Zena lacks in other areas, she makes up for in heart.

I think back now to her supposed caretakers saying "Who would want her?" and I am profoundly sad. Not for Zena, because she now has all that a dog, companion, member of MY family could ever ask for. I feel sad for her former family. For a man who could not see the value of a dog, the love that waited to be shared at any moment with just a kind touch and a scratch under the chin. For the wife who did not shed a tear for the faithful friend who had spent seventeen years with her family.

But the saddest part was the cold lesson those kids learned that freezing January day. When something gets old, when the toy has lost its shine, you just throw it away. I wonder how these kids are going to handle their parents when they become old? Maybe the same way the parents dealt with Zena?

They said there is no value to an old dog, well I say they have it all wrong. I say Zena is a priceless gem, a jewel, a diamond that I am proud to add to the safe deposit box that is my heart.

Zena kisses Joe, her savior, on the day he came for her

Wendy Fights
for Wendell

BY SHARI STRADER, DDB NORTH CAROLINA REP

℘

I first heard about Wendell from Wendy, the neighbor who lived across the street from him. She emailed me and I could tell from her description that his situation was dire. I drove out to see him and knew right away that something had to be done.

He was chained with a giant tow truck chain that was padlocked around his neck. His dog house was in two pieces, he had no food, no water, and he was skinny . . . very skinny.

In her letter to me, Wendy described Wendell's situation. She said she would occasionally get a glimpse of him pacing while on his chain, and she noticed that he was thin, so she started to keep a close watch on him. Fear of retribution towards her cats by Wendell's owner kept her quiet until the situation deteriorated to a point that she could stand it no more.

Wendy knew Wendell didn't have adequate shelter and after a severe rainstorm, she had had enough and called animal control to look at the situation. The visit by animal control had no visible impact on Wendell's situation other than the owner moving him so she could no longer see him from the street. Wendy could hear him barking, and it was even worse wondering how he was each day.

Her opportunity to observe him finally came when the neighbors next to Wendell's house moved. Wendy was able to see him over the fence and it was the saddest sight she had ever seen. He had lost a significant amount of weight since she'd last seen him and it was obvious to her that he was going to starve to death if something wasn't done.

She was disillusioned with animal control and had no intention of calling them again but yet knew something had to be done to save Wendell. She decided the situation called for drastic measures and if she could find a home for Wendell, she would take him to save his life.

Until then, she would sneak over every night and throw him food over the fence. At first, he would bark and then move away and only after she left would he devour the food. After a few times, he knew she was a friend and stopped barking and started wagging his tail in anticipation of the food whenever he saw her.

About two weeks into her search for a new home for Wendell, she heard about Dogs Deserve Better and thought, let this organization be the answer to my prayers . . . and it was. She called me and the very same day I was over there documenting and photographing the abuse.

It nearly took an act of Congress to get Wendell out of his neglectful and abusive home. First I contacted a friend who knew the animal control director in this county and she made a call to get animal control over there again . . . and again; each time animal control left without Wendell and nothing changed.

After several more calls to animal control and a statement from a veterinarian about the condition of the dog, animal control finally seized Wendell. My friend was able to get him out of the shelter and into a temporary foster home.

Wendell tested positive for heartworms and was emaciated, but other than that he was in OK shape. His first foster home didn't work out, so we set about trying to find another place for him to go. I came across a rescuer in Maryland who was more than happy to take him in, so Wendy (the neighbor who originally called me) took a road trip to Maryland to drop him off and meet his new family. He made it through his heartworm treatments just fine and was finally placed in a forever home.

Even though Wendell was terribly neglected, his spirit was alive and he liked to play. At his abusive home, all he had to play with was an old tire and his empty water bucket. Even later when he was safe and had toys around, he still wanted to play with his water bowls. Now he has all the toys his heart desires.

If it weren't for Wendy and her determination to save this dog, I doubt he'd be alive today.

Some People
Call Me Gordi

BY BELEN BRISCO, DDB FLORIDA REP

⅋

Gordi, in his "call me Gordon" pose

I go by several different names; each one is used in a loving way so I don't care that they are different. Some people call me Gordi, my foster mom calls me Gord, and my foster dad calls me Gordon. I like that. I was told that I bit someone and that was a very big mistake. They can make you go to sleep for good for doing something like that. I didn't know the guy and he was yanking at my collar and not being very nice. You see, I had just been adopted by a new family and I hadn't had the opportunity to meet all of them. I guess this was "his" room and "his" bed. I didn't know.

Next thing I know it looks like I have to go back to the shelter because my adopted family doesn't want me anymore. Now, the people at the shelter were very nice but I just wanted to have a home of my own. The lady who rescued me couldn't take me home and there wasn't anyplace else for me to go.

Then all of the sudden, Belen Brisco, a Dogs Deserve Better representative, said she would take me and foster me. She had met me before at the shelter; it turns out we had actually had a few walks together. So, next thing I know, I'm being picked up and taken to the vet. I heard my new foster mom talking to the vet and saying she wanted to make sure I wasn't in any pain anywhere before she began her work with me. I'm thinking I'm going to like her.

The vet gave me a big thumbs up! She said that I am a great-looking dog for being seven years old and that I am in good shape and downright handsome, too. Ok, she might have said "good looking," I can't remember, but I do know I liked her treats.

She said something about being "hand shy." That maybe I had not been treated kindly and so I was fearful of quick hand movements. The shelter didn't have any real record of my past, other than I was a stray, but they thought I probably came from a bad life where I was chained or treated badly. Now that we have a good idea of what might have gone wrong, my foster mom is calling in a dog trainer to work with us.

I like her too; her name is Lynn. Lynn is going to be coming over every Monday to spend time with me. My foster mom has a nice place for me to stay and has learned that crates and thunderstorms are not my favorite thing. She actually slept downstairs with me for ten nights! I am feeling more comfortable and have moved from behind the couch to my doggy bed in front of the couch. Little steps like this make my foster mom so happy. They make me happy too. I feel like I am wanted here and the whole family works me with.

We take walks in the morning with the other dogs. Man, are they lucky to live here full time; Border Collies, Great Pyrenees and now a Shepherd mix, that's me. Mom and dad say we look like a circus coming down the street. I think we look like a good looking pack of dogs.

We all get to rest for a bit after our walk in the morning and then we get our food. Play time is hanging out with the pack and watching them catch the ball and other toys. I haven't yet picked up the knack of toys. Maybe I didn't have any before, but it sure looks like fun.

Mom and dad pick up all the toys when we are through and then I get to hang out in mom's office while she works.

The storms still bother me and I shake a bit but maybe one day I will get over that. Mom and dad think I must have been left outside in the rain and dark because I am afraid of both.

It has been three weeks and I am doing very well with my training and have showed no signs of aggression at all. I am a sweet guy; a gentleman, mom and dad call me. I just started public dog training to get to meet other dogs and people for exposure. I went to my first meet and greet class last week and it was great. *I* was great!

Maybe someone will fall in love with me and want me for their forever pet. I sure would like to stay where I am, but I know that I am very adoptable and that it is soon going to be time for me to make room for another poor pup that might need a second chance. The shelter is even going to post my picture on their website to help me get adopted again. I am praying that I get someone who is patient and kind and doesn't mind if I am not a young pup anymore.

I am calm, gentle and very loving. What more could a pack leader want? Thank you Dogs Deserve Better for giving me a second chance. Where would I be without you?

Sadie and Mikey
Weren't Sweethearts

BY PATRICIA ALDERING, DDB MICHIGAN REP

ༀ

Mikey, in a rare moment of rest at his new home

Sadie and Mikey are Beagles who we rescued during a snow storm. A local news story convinced their caretaker to contact Dogs Deserve Better to relinquish two chained dogs. It was not an easy place to get to as Kelly, one of my volunteers, and I maneuvered our vehicles down long snow covered rural roads through yet another snow storm. We got lost but eventually found ourselves at a house that sat back off the road. The cold was numbing; my lips were so cold I could barely talk and I could not feel my fingers. Unfortunately, these poor dogs had no choice but to live outdoors in this harsh weather.

According to the guardian, Sadie was used for breeding and was chained during the day but brought inside at night (I've heard that one before). She was seven years old and graying.

Mikey, one of her offspring, was young and very thin. His chain was so short that he could barely move.

We had to get the Beagles out because the snow was accumulating quickly and it was rapidly getting dark. Kelly and I decided that we needed to make the 45-minute trek home as soon as possible before conditions became unmanageable. Kelly loaded Mikey into her car and I put Sadie into mine for the trip home. Unfortunately, we ended up getting stuck backing out of the driveway. The owner loaned us shovels and returned inside while we eventually dug ourselves out.

As we pulled out into the road, I could see Mikey jumping up and down on the backseat of Kelly's car while trying to look out the rear window. It was quite comical, almost as if he was leaping for joy at the thought of never seeing that backyard again. Sadie whined the whole way home which I found out was her modus operandi; she would whine unceasingly for no apparent reason. We were able to break her of that habit very quickly, thank goodness, and now she only whines when she wants food.

Sadie and Mikey both tested positive for heartworm but are now healthy and enjoying their new-found freedom. Sadie loves to hide bones and won't use just any old spot. She will search diligently to find the perfect spot for her bone. We have found them tucked inside her dog bed, under piles of laundry, and even under our pillows!

Mikey's foster family adopted Mikey and report that he enjoys tearing through the house, and chasing and playing tug-of-war with their foster dogs.

What a difference in both of these beautiful babies since we rescued them from that frozen backyard on a cold and wintry Minnesota day. I know if they could speak, their thanks would fill volumes.

She Was Left
for Dead

BY GAYLA FRANCES EVANS, DDB OHIO REP

℘

Sadee, a beautiful girl now that she's recovered

This is a story about a dog who was chained and left to die. It is a story about a beautiful girl who was neglected for life by a thoughtless guardian. It is a story about how the kindness and love of many different people made a rescue happen. It is a story about Sadee.

Often times the rescue of an animal is the work of a group of people rather than just one person. It is the group of people, often complete strangers to one another, who share a compassion for animals and are drawn together by a special need. In Sadee's case, it started off with the kindness of a utility worker who saw the conditions that Sadee and another dog were living in and who had the fortitude to report the abuse to the proper authorities.

It took Dog Warden Dave Speakman of Richland County Shelter to go out to find Sadee in high weeds with no path to where she was being kept on her heavy chain and only a wood box with a hole in it for shelter. Sadee was nothing more than a skeleton, had given up, and was dying on her chain. She had suffered for years at the hands of a guardian who was severely negligent in her responsibilities to provide a loving and caring home for Sadee.

It took Lori Miller of Richland County Shelter who couldn't believe her eyes when Sadee was brought into the shelter. Sadee weighed barely 21 pounds, and was severely dehydrated and emaciated. Sadee was beyond living, her paws were folded under which is a sure sign she was close to death, so weak and frail she couldn't stand or even hold her head up. Lori held her head and gave her a small amount of food though she wouldn't take a drink. Lori took Sadee to her vet, who gave her a blood transfusion and IVs.

By some miracle, within 48 hours, Sadee started eating and drinking on her own. Lori then took her home for some tender loving care, which included a gentle bath to cleanse her soiled fur.

It took Dogs Deserve Better representative Gayla Frances Evans to take Sadee into her home as a foster and provide her with the love and care she so desperately lacked the first part of her life.

Sadee doubled her weight within three weeks and reached 50 pounds in no time, quickly gaining a great appetite and disposition.

This was a perfect example of the absolute worst-case scenario for a dog living on a chain. Sadee wasn't a pet; she was a prisoner to her life on the chain, with no regular food, water, care, love and most of all no choice. There is no doubt in my mind that Sadee wouldn't have made it even one more day; she was dying plain and simple.

You would think that this was an open-shut case for animal abuse charges but no charges were filed on the previous guardian because she was in her late 70's. To top it all off, not only was she not charged but she had the audacity to ask for Sadee back! Not in my lifetime.

Sadee is the happy ending to a truly horrible story. But there were two dogs the utility worker saw that day hidden in high weeds. Sadee was able to be saved, but just barely, the other one had to be euthanized.

I hope anyone who knows of older people who have dogs will make an effort to check on them and their dogs more often so they don't end up like Sadee and her companion.

I am truly grateful for all those that took part in saving Sadee with a special thank you to Lori Miller and her vet for going that extra mile.

Update on Sadee:

It's been two years since Sadee was rescued and what a joy she has been; she's made an unbelievable transformation.

Her favorite toy is a huge plastic orange ball that she hits with her paw and bark at as long as you let her. We call her Squeaky Sadee because she sounds like a squeak toy when she barks; it's quite humorous. Even if you can't see her, you know she found her ball when you hear her squeak constantly.

Sadee is about 55 to 60 pounds now, a big difference from just over 21 pounds when I got her. She still has a great appetite, and enjoys every day to the fullest.

Sadee always has a smile on her face and a nub that wiggles nonstop; she's a very loving girl. Because of her age she will probably live her life out here with the rest of the seniors, but I really don't mind and neither does she.

Everyone who meets her falls in love with her. Maybe someday fate will step in and that special someone will want to adopt her and give her the love she never had but surely deserves. In the meantime, she can squeak her heart out with her big orange ball and enjoy life. Sadee will always have a forever home here.

His Name is
Nate the Great

BY MARION HEWKO, BRITISH COLUMBIA REP

ℬ

Nate gets his photo with Santa

Pauline has been working with and donating dog food to the First Nations communities (Native reserves) up north for the last two years. She had heard of Dogs Deserve Better by googling the internet and found my telphone number. We started talking on the telephone often, and before long she asked me if I wanted to come with her to help feed the dogs, deworm them, and to look at this feral dog who was apparently very scared and very skinny. The dog was always looking for food, but nobody would feed her.

Pauline and I stayed with her sister, who is an R.N. and also works with the First Nations people. After spending the night, we drove up the dirt and gravel road carrying walkie-talkies—there is no cell phone reception—and were greeted by the kids of the village, excitedly talking and wanting to know all about us.

The first thing we did was stop and feed the dogs, who were running all over the road, puppies in tow. They were all so hungry and after they ate and left, we saw a white dog coming out of the forest, shy as can be, head down, and skinny . . . oh, so skinny.

She found some left-over kibble from the other dogs, and we crouched down closer to her to feed her more; but even though she wanted to, she was so scared, and took off back into the woods. Even the other dogs chased her away when she came back after a little while.

She was so beautiful—yes she was skinny—but she had a beautiful white coat and her ears were large with one that flopped over while one stood up straight. We called her Nayla, which means "White Spirit."

We tried to catch her by putting food in the van, but she was smarter than us, and she jumped back out of the van, over and over. She was so quick.

We dewormed all the puppies and the adult dogs, we educated the people on how to care for the dogs—not to chain them, of course—but also to provide loving indoor homes, and to spay and neuter them, which they were obviously in great need of.

We had a few people who really loved and did right by their dogs, and they promised us to keep an eye out for all the dogs.

After two days of trying to catch Nayla, we had to go home, but not empty handed. No, we didn't manage to catch Nayla, but we did bring five puppies back with us, who were vetted and adopted out into loving homes within weeks.

After another two months, Pauline again went up to the community with two other volunteers, and sure enough, Nayla was still there. She was still skinny, still feral, but now her fur did not look good at all; she was very sick, and yet she would not come close to humans.

After two days of trying to trap her, her "sister" Ginger went into the van first and—guess what!—Nayla jumped in the van, the doors were quickly closed, and the long trip to freedom, vet care and a loving foster home began!

When Nayla got to the vet, we had to lift the trap out of the van, as we were so scared that Nayla would bolt had we tried to leash her. At the vet's we were told that Nayla was NO GIRL, she was a BOY! We had no idea, she just didn't look like a boy to us.

The vet determined that he was very emaciated, and was covered in mange and fleas. Nayla could not be neutered as he was way to weak, so we decided to wait until he was stronger. The foster people also loved his sister Ginger and wanted to foster both dogs. The day after the mange dip and flea treatment Nayla was released into the fosters' care and they worked miracles with him and Ginger. He gained weight, and learned what love and trust was.

In August, the mange came back and Nayla looked worse than he had before. Then we received word that the foster parents' lives had dramatically changed and they could not look after the two dogs anymore. We were told that Nayla was very sick and the foster parents wanted to euthanize him.

"No way!" we said, and picked Nayla and Ginger up that day.

Nayla looked horrible! His skin was flaky, and what little hair he had left was dry and falling out. He had been neutered a few months prior, and our vet thought that surgery compromised his immune system and he developed mange again.

Poor Nayla had to endure the skin scrape again, and was shaved bald—he was such a pitiful looking dog!

Our vet, Dr. Mann, was a godsend; he allowed us to board Nayla with them for seven long weeks. He became the poster dog for the clinic because every moment possible someone was working with him, touching him, feeding him, walking him. He did so well.

We then decided he had a new leash on life, so we changed his name to Nate. He went into an awesome foster home, and then we got a few applications of people interested in adopting Nate.

There was one couple that stood out. One of the positives was that they lived only two minutes from my house, so I was able to see Nate often. The homecheck went great and when we dropped Nate off, he walked in like he lived there all his life!

His hair started to grow back and by Christmas he was this gorgeous white dog. When he came for the Santa picture fundraiser for Dogs Deserve Better and saw me, he just howled and I cried. Happy tears for him, but also sad tears for every thing he had gone through.

His name is Nate The Great, and that HE is.

Why Every Man Wants to
Date or Marry a DDB Rep

BY TAMIRA CI THAYNE, FOUNDER, DOGS DESERVE BETTER

ℬ

Tami and Joe, on a romantic walk with Banshee in tow

I have a boyfriend now, which might amaze you as much as it amazes me. I was pretty much under the impression that it would be a cold day in Hades before I'd ever be dating again.

Not that I'm especially ugly or anything, but I couldn't imagine that any man in his right mind would want to date me because my life is incredibly hectic—mostly due to Dogs Deserve Better—and I currently house anywhere from 4-8 dogs at a time, and from 8-12 cats at a time. Not to mention the two kids that come and go, and the DDB employees and volunteers who are in and out.

I'm obligation-laden . . . which is anything but sexy.

The bright side—if there is one—is that like most animal rescue ladies I have an exceptionally warm heart and an exceptionally warm bed (courtesy of the four dog heaters strategically placed at all four corners).

That's gotta' count for something in the dead of winter, at least.

Dating a rescuer can be fraught with perils, both emotional and physical, for any intrepid would-be suitor. For example, take this recent hike to the woods for some couple-time with my beau. In theory it sounds sweet and romantic, right?

I suppose it could have turned out that way, even with the five dogs I drag along, if it weren't for a few unforeseen incidents which wiped out any romantic notions we may have been having.

ᵷ

Joe, my sweetheart of eight months, asks me before we go if I'm SURE I want to take Weston—the new fox terrier pup who has a slight inclination to get car sick and absolutely HATES cars—along on the hike with the other four fosters.

I answer with an affirmative "Yes! If he starts to associate car rides with fun things like hikes in the woods with his pack, he'll stop hating the car and therefore stop getting carsick. Besides, it's only two miles up the road, and even Weston can't barf that quickly."

In hindsight, feeding him breakfast just 1/2 hour before leaving might not have been the most brilliant of plans.

No sooner do we reach the stop sign at a mile, than I hear a *whoosh* which could only be the sound of dog puke being projectiled and then hitting, well, *something*. And then, *whoosh*, again.

I can't get a good look back there, since I'm driving and all, but I immediately imagine exactly where the puke landed; other dogs, the blanket, the mats under the blanket, or—worst case scenario—the van carpet and between the cracks in the floor.

I quickly toss aside my goody-two-shoes plan for getting Weston used to the car, and pull out the demon-vow which goes along the lines of "I will never drive that dog anywhere ever again, period. He will rot in my house for the rest of his life or until I sucker someone into adopting him, but he will never step foot into my vehicle again."

Mind you, I can't literally accomplish this since I can't leave him in the woods (can I?) and will actually have to drive him back to my house in an hour—thereby instantly blowing my vow—but it feels good to have a plan of action, anyway.

When we get to the woods I immediately observe that it *is* worst-case scenario and then some. There is still-warm slightly-used dog-gie-kibble on the blanket, the mats, the other dogs, AND oozing its way into every crack and crevice of the vehicle.

How romantic are you feeling about now? Yeah, so are we.

So we drag out the blanket and let it lay on the ground to deal with on the return trip. I grab a towel from the front and use it to mop up some of the wettest stuff, shake it out, and then we carry it and the two mats with us down to the stream to wash off the biggest chunks before heading back into the woods.

As luck would have it, just as we start toward the stream with our booty, another car pulls up with a photographer and a family on board, who all proceed to get out and head in the same direction to capture the fall family portrait. Great!

This is my off-leash woods, where no one usually goes but me and the dogs, so all are running free, and Joe and I have our hands full doing the 'laundry' in the stream like good pioneer folk.

The photography people stop at the other side of the stream, and I grab Banshee because he's the one most-inclined to consider a good bite. Only one dog actually goes over and tries to get some lovin'—you guessed it—Weston.

Admittedly, Weston DOES have a cute little puppy face

My nemesis.

Weston, a very young, cute dog, tends to bring out the puppy lover in everyone with his innocent eyes and whimsical face—except these people, apparently.

They are yelling "Come get your puke-infested dog," (Ok, I added the puke-infested part) while Joe is knee deep in barf-mat and barf-towel and I'm struggling to hang onto Banshee and remove chunkage from the second mat.

We quickly drop the mats and make a bee-line to the trail in order to lure Weston away from his haters. It works, and Joe and I try to entomb the memories of what we've just endured and get back into the spirit of togetherness, exercise, and couple time.

We make it to the top of the mountain without incident, but on the way back down suddenly realize we're missing Delilah. Delilah, a Shepherd mix, rarely leaves our immediate vicinity because she's sight-impaired, and often runs into branches and other trail-side appendages. She feels more secure knowing we're nearby.

This is cause for concern.

Joe says he'll backtrack to look for her, while I stay put in case she just wandered off the trail temporarily and comes back seeking us. About twenty feet behind me, Joe stops and picks something up from the ground.

What's that, I wonder.

"Drop something, honey?" He calls sweetly. "You should thank Delilah for this," he says, as he pockets the keys to my van which have somehow, secretly and unbeknownst to me, fallen out of my pocket noiselessly onto the trail. "We would not have been happy searching every inch of trail for these later."

I try the old "I'm pretty sure you were carrying them, dear," trick, innocently, with a bat of the eyelashes, but he wasn't falling for it, and I got our standard "Uh huh" in reply, which is what we use when we know the other is full of crap and they know that we know it too. Or something like that.

Delilah and friends Quest and Banshee walking in the woods

We spend 1/2 hour searching the woods near and far for Delilah, and just as we decide to head back to the car to see if she's waiting there, I spot her nonchalantly walking off the bank and onto the trail ahead.

"Delilah!" I yell, so happy to see her. She guiltily starts and looks about before joining the pack, pretending she's been there the whole time.

"Honey," I say, "Doesn't it look like she has something all over her back?"

And then a dim, dark memory from long ago, an era before Dogs Deserve Better, surfaces from the far reaches of my cobwebbed brain. It's of a time without responsibility, before a fence, when my two dogs used to run the neighborhood and woods behind my house. Not only did they find themselves trouble with porcupines, skunks, and various and sundry other live critters, but one of their favorite things to do was to find any old dead animal and roll in it.

"Oh, shit," I exclaim, in a most unladylike fashion, as the realization dawns on me.

"What is it now?" he says, the stress starting to take a toll on his normally placid demeanor.

"Dead animal." I stoop down to take a whiff, even though I know in advance what I'm going to smell. The unmistakable stench hits me before my nose gets a foot from her back. "Yep. She found something dead, and she's been back there rolling this whole time."

We shuffle along back toward the van, silently, defeated, all zest for hiking (and romance!) squelched. We gather up the mats and blanket, load the crew, and come on back home.

Yes, we bring Weston, too.

I spend the next hour bathing Delilah with our brand-new Stinky Dog shampoo, and scrubbing the yak out of the carpet threads, crevices, and seats of the van.

The glamour of my job never ends.

I know Joe has to wonder what the hell happened to him at times.

If he's smart he wishes for a 'normal' girlfriend, one who works 9-5 Monday-Friday, cooks him dinner at night, and snuggles on the couch reading a book beside him on weekends.

Who can blame him?

Instead, what he has is a woman with a mission, a woman with some serious baggage, and a woman for whom life is rarely dull.

The truth is we animal rescuers are NOT easy women to date for the average man—the man who wants the easy way out, the man who has no compassion for fur-bearing creatures, the man who has no respect for women who stand tall.

But for that rare gem of a man who values strength, courage, kindness, and sincerity, you've come to the right place. Because we animal rescuers are the most courageous bunch of women on the planet, and we deserve not only good men and true partners in our lives, but great men and worthy partners.

Come on in, guys. The water isn't warm, dinner is not on the table, but there is that warm heart and warm bed thing to consider.

And who wanted life to be boring, anyway?

How DDB Reps (and You!) Influence Others for Animals:
Yes, I Saved a Turtle

BY JOSEPH HORVATH, FLEDGLING ANIMAL ADVOCATE

℘

Let me start by saying that not all stories have happy endings. This one does, but sometimes in order to experience that happy ending you have to experience sadness along the way first . . .

And it's not a story about saving a dog, either, as that hasn't happened to me yet. Instead, it's a story about how I learned that animals, not just dogs, do matter.

My girlfriend, Tami, and I were driving to Florida to surprise her best friend Tracy for her engagement party. We were in a convertible Mustang with the top down running 80 mph in the center lane of I-95—quite an enjoyable experience for me, to be sure.

Now I understood that Tami loves animals but I didn't know until this trip just how much. As I said, we were driving down I-95 when we passed a turtle attempting to cross the six-lane highway; not such a smart move on his/her part. I was instructed to stop and go back.

Ok, she yelled it at me but then the top was down so she probably had to, right? It took me about 1/2 mile or so to get stopped and over to the side of the road. I backed up and backed up until we were a mere 100 feet from saving this poor misguided turtle, but as it turned out we were 100 feet too late.

A sadistic trucker decided today was the day he was going to take out an innocent creature, and he deliberately ran over the turtle, which was at that time on the dotted line and should have been safe.

Tami was devastated. She could not stop picturing that poor turtle, and she asked me to catch up to the offending trucker so she could give him a piece of her mind. After catching him, Tami uttered a significant amount of choice words to the driver (with associated hand gestures), and I vowed no turtle would die on my watch again.

Fast forward to six weeks or so later and we are again rolling down the highway, although this time it's a four lane highway heading out of D.C. We are less than a mile from the traffic light when I see a turtle in our lane attempting to cross the road.

I spring into action by immediately slamming on the brakes and pulling over without so much as a sideways glance at Tami. As I'm backing up I see the light change and two lanes of traffic start accelerating toward the turtle. I decide today is not his (or her…I mean really, how can you tell) day to die as memories of Florida flash through my mind.

I throw the van into park, jump out, and grab that turtle, getting us both off the highway right before the two lanes of traffic come hurtling by. After all the cars go by I carry the turtle across four lanes of traffic and over the guardrail and take him (or her…I mean really) down to a little creek.

Now, I will admit I didn't scope out the whole situation when I grabbed that turtle and I am feeling pretty good about my save when I get back to the van—that is until Tami asks me which way the turtle was heading.

Now, I will also admit that I might have made some assumptions in regards to which way he (or she . . . I mean really) was going. They are round…right? It's not like they are shaped like an arrow.

I assumed he was ONE lane into crossing the four-lane highway. I didn't consider that he might have been THREE lanes into crossing the highway and I put him (or her…I mean really) back at the starting point.

I'm going to stick with my gut feeling on this and say that turtle was at the start of the journey and I truly did save him (or her…I mean really) a whole lot of footwork and a possible early demise crossing that highway.

It's what lets me sleep at night.

Why Dogs Deserve Better?
How I Became a DDB Rep

BY DAWN ASHBY, DDB ILLINOIS REP

ℰ

Dawn lovin' on her favorite boy, Romeo

Chained since puppyhood, the Lab mix next door grew up isolated, alone, and living in mud and feces. Many of our neighbors called animal control, the police, anyone they could think of, but when someone came to investigate, we were always told there weren't existing laws to help. He was confined to the property, he was alive so someone was feeding and watering him, and he had a doghouse for shelter.

One summer, the Department of Agriculture instructed me not to feed or water the skinny black dog and they would arrive in eight days to check his condition. I couldn't do it. I continued to feed him and give him water, which interfered with the investigation. As he grew restless on the chain, he became increasingly aggressive. He bit a child cutting across the yard to visit a friend, but not severely. Eventually I was the only one who could approach him.

He thought he was my dog. Chained dogs are often placed faraway from a caregiver's home, out of sight and out of mind. He was next to my property line and became excited when he saw me pull into the drive. He never made a sound when his caregivers returned.

Once he broke free and came straight to my door. "I'm home!" his expression and wagging tail told me. "I made it! I'm home!" A part of me died when his guardian came to retrieve him that day.

I purchased many toys and bones for him to ease his boredom. My husband teased me about being the only person who would sneak over to the neighbor's yard after dark to give flea baths to their dog in the summer and put straw in his doghouse in the winter. One sunny afternoon another neighbor was playing with their yellow Lab in an adjacent yard, tossing a toy for Duke to retrieve. I watched Black Dog as he went through the pile of toys I had purchased for him. He rooted around in them until he came up with the exact duplicate of the toy Duke was fetching.

I watched with my own eyes as Black Dog held that toy in his mouth, a slow wag of his tail rocking from side to side as he stood on his circle of dry ground, watching the neighbor play with his dog. He even tossed the toy into the air and caught it on his own to make his point. It would be a day that changed my life.

Black Dog understood, he understood he wanted a family, he understood he wanted to play, he understood he didn't want to be chained, he longed to be part of something, part of someone, to live a life where people would toss a toy for him to fetch. He understood and I knew he understood. My heart was still pounding when I went into the house. With my hand on the receiver of the phone I knew I had to call someone. "Dear Lord, please, I need to call someone, who can help him?"

Then I lifted my hand away from the telephone. Sadly, there was no one to call. The reality was no one would help. In that same moment yet another truth presented itself to me, "I AM someone. I AM the someone who can help."

I had no idea how I was going to go about this, but I was determined. I searched the Internet and found www.dogsdeservebetter. org. I wasn't alone, there was a whole website describing exactly how I felt. It was early on, and DDB was little more than a twinkle in Tami's eye, but it connected me with others, and gave me the information and strength I needed.

Since that day, I have rescued Black Dog and hundreds of other backyard dogs. More than 200 of them have been fostered in my home and adopted to forever inside families. Many more just like him have been rescued and fostered in the homes of representatives and volunteers.

Over the years, I've cheered with every law change against 24/7 chaining. I've watched as other organizations joined in our fight. I've cried with Tami as she struggled through trials imposed on her because of her compassion and dedication. Creating Dogs Deserve Better and taking a stand for the neglected backyard dog opened her to adversities with finances, family, friends, enemies, and the courts.

I've felt pride in Tami's growing strength. I've made an amazing friend in her, and I love her dearly. My heart swelled when her partner Joe came along and swept her off her feet. Yes, sometimes-even rescuers need rescued. For the first time Tami's eyes sparkle and she has a warmer, more peaceful smile. I've had the privilege to read her first book, *Scream Like Banshee*, which empowered me to forgive myself and improve.

I'm indebted to Dogs Deserve Better and Tamira Ci Thayne. I owe my life to a 24/7-chained, skinny mixed breed, forgotten backyard dog. Black Dog helped me find my voice, my purpose. He changed me from a helpless, silent, neighbor to an outgoing advocate for animals. I will never feel small, insignificant, or silent again. I am someone who is making a difference.

Martin Luther King Jr. said, "Our lives begin to end the day we become silent about things that matter." For you and me . . . our lives begin the day we break our silence about things that matter. The lives of chained and penned backyard dogs will start when they cease to exist as pieces of unwanted, unloved, forgotten property and become valued as part of the family.

This will only happen because of people like Tami, because of all the area representatives of Dogs Deserve Better, because of donors and members who give generously to the cause.

Change will happen when people like you and me refuse to remain silent about this socially acceptable form of cruelty. Dog chaining hits us where we live, in our cities and small towns. Together we can end the suffering that has been an accepted norm of our society for far too long.

Visit Dogs Deserve Better to discover how to make a difference in a chained dogs life.

You can do this. You are someone who can break chains.

A Memorial to Area Rep
Tamar Sherman

DDB CALIFORNIA REP

℘

April 27, 1971 - May 9, 2007

Tamar Sherman, daughter of Catherine Gidos Sherman and Yehuda Sherman of Lafayette, California, was born April 27, 1971, and lost her three-year battle with breast cancer on May 9, 2007, at the young age of 36.

Tamar was a tireless advocate for abused and neglected animals, and a sales administration specialist for a medical supply company.

When DDB founder Tamira Thayne, posted this statement, "It's with a sad heart that I tell you all that California area rep Tamar Sherman passed away May 9th, losing her fight with breast cancer," a silence fell as we all knew there would forever be a hole left in animal rescue that could only be filled by Tamar.

She was named "Remarkable Rep of the Year, 2006" in voting by her fellow Dogs Deserve Better area reps.

At 32 years old, her arrest for "petting a dog and giving it water" shocked dog lovers across the nation when it was released by the Associated Press, and her story was blogged all over the internet.

Tamar was an instrumental piece in the passing of the three-hour California tethering limit, representing Dogs Deserve Better in the California Animal Alliance. Her efforts to save chained dogs made the news in San Jose and other parts of California.

Tamar worked to free chained dogs until the very end.

Said Tamar's mom, Catherine Sherman, "She was so touched to be nominated as Area Rep of the Year that she cried; she also cried when she wrote her letter of resignation, and the work of this group-—DDB—meant so very much to her."

Tamar, we love you and we miss you, and we think of you as we continue our fight to bring dogs out of backyards and into the home and family. We *will not stop!*

Acknowledgments

&

This book is by and for Dogs Deserve Better reps, and all those who support our efforts and believe too that all dogs deserve to live inside with the family. Hold firm to our collective vision!

We first and foremost want to thank our reps, who work this issue every day, take their volunteer rolls seriously, and make it happen in their communities. Without you the cause of chaining would be still at the starting gate. With you, we are rounding the first bend!

Thank you for taking even more time out of your busy lives to sit down and write your unique rescue tales. Much appreciated.

Next, we are incredibly grateful to our donors, who've kept us going since 2002, even in times of bad economy. You all believe in our mission, you believe in our work, and you continue to show us your love time and time again. We love you right back!

I can truly say without you we would not be here.

A big book-thanks to Joe Horvath, who deserves to be listed as a third editor for all the proofing and re-proofing he did on the book. As always, we rush to deadline, and with his help we've done our best to make the book as error-free and professional as possible. (We know you're lookin' for errors now, and you'll probably find some! Do us a favor, though, and pretend you don't see any. Thanks!)

Lastly, we'd like to acknowledge and thank the local hard-working anti-chaining groups which have sprung up around the country. Groups such as PAWSitive Effects, Coalition to Unchain Dogs, Chain Free Austin, ChainFree Asheville, Chain Free Beaufort and others recently formed or forming as we write are doing their share to show chaining the door. Both the dogs you serve and Dogs Deserve Better thank you.

About Dogs Deserve Better

§

Dogs Deserve Better, 2003 First Place Winner of the ASPCA/Chase Pet Protector Award, is a voice for chained and penned dogs, whose sadness speaks only through the eyes. As the days become years, many of these dogs sit, lay, eat, and defecate within the same 10-foot radius. Chained by the neck, they exist without respect, love, exercise, social interaction, and sometimes even basic nourishment. They live as prisoners, yet long to be pets.

Chaining is not only inhumane for dogs, but has taken a severe toll on this nation's children as well. In the period from October 2003 through October 2009, there were at least 283 children killed or seriously injured by chained dogs across the country. Chained dogs, unsocialized with humans, can become very territorial of their tiny space, and any two year old who wanders into this space can be attacked and killed before adults can intervene.

Would you for one second choose to live the life of these dogs? No matter what reason is given, the bottom line is that it is NOT acceptable to chain a dog for life. Dogs should not have to live chained or penned as prisoners, yearning for a place in a family, craving acknowledgement, respect, and love. They DESERVE BETTER, and we as caretakers have the obligation to provide it for them.

Please consider today how you can help the dogs in your neighborhood. If you see a chained dog or a penned dog daily, it is time to take action. Please join Dogs Deserve Better today in taking a stand against this mistreatment of dogs. Donate, volunteer, or read more at:

www.dogsdeservebetter.org

Editor Photo by Darin Ashby

About the Editor

Dawn Ashby was raised by wolves in Central Illinois. All right, not wolves exactly, but the Wolfe's did raise her, as this is her maiden name. As a rescuer, she has volunteered with United Animal Nations during Hurricane Katrina, and for many non-profit rescues including Illinois Dalmatian Rescue.

She has served as long-time representative for Dogs Deserve Better, and while Rescue and Public Liaison Director, was interviewed and quoted in numerous articles, and has written many articles on the subject of backyard dogs and the hazards of dog chaining. A freelance writer presently working on her own novel, she resides in Litchfield, Illinois, with husband Darin. They have three daughters, Michelle, Brittany and Alyssa. Dawn shares her life with her fluffy constant, Romeo the Saint Bernard, and the furry souls rescued from lives on chains.

She's still sadly missing her best friend and family Dalmatian, Spectre, who crossed the bridge in 2008. Dawn rules her canine kingdom with a lint roller in one hand and wine glass in the other. C'est la vie!

About the Editor

Tamira Ci Thayne is founder and CEO of Dogs Deserve Better, an award-winning national nonprofit working on behalf of America's chained and penned dogs.

Thayne holds a B.A. in Visual Arts from the University of Maryland, and a B.S. and M.S. in Naturology (study of the Body/Mind/Spirit connection) from American Institute of Holistic Theology.

She has written articles for nationwide publications including *American Dog*, and has been the subject of articles in magazines such as *Bark*, *Animal Sheltering*, *The New Barker*, and *Dog's Life*, which won a Genesis Award Honorable Mention.

She is the author of *Scream Like Banshee: 29 Days of Tips and Tales to Keep Your Sanity as a Doggie Foster Parent*, and the illustrator of *Puddles on the Floor* for Dogs Deserve Better, a humane education book written by Lorena Estep. She has created over 30 animal advocacy art pieces, available for viewing and purchase on littlegirllooking.com, as well as the best-selling Animal Rescue Angel tattoo design.

Sponsors:

℘

This book was made possible, in part, by the organizations and personal sponsors listed here. We are very grateful for their generous donations for printing costs, so that more of the purchase price can go directly to education of caretakers, fencing programs, and vetting and rehoming of chained dogs.

Lilith Aquino
Dawn Beattie
JoAnne Berg
Judy Black
Suzanne Bowles
Russell Brinton
Belen Brisco
Carol S Brown
Melanie Browne-Klein
Barbara Bryan
William Burgess
Marcia Byers
Shannon S. Campbell
Deb, Rich, & Dylan Carr
Pam Cheatham
Kathy Chilton
Mary Chipman
Cynthia Clark
Dawn Marie Clarkson
Lisa Compton
Kathleen Conroy
Patty Crocker
Sharon M. Darr
Kelley Dickey
Irene Dorang
Marjorie Dorbolo
Veronica Doster-Booth

Lynn Dourourips
Naomi Egami
Kathleen Engberg
Lorena & Charles Estep
Patricia Fellenbaum
Debbie Fields
Jan Fields
Elaine Gaynor
Darrell Jay Gilbert
Carol Giles-Straight
Karen Goodman
Rose, Gary, and Mollie Gordon
Penelope A Gummo
Sherrie Hamilton
Sherri Hand
Lori Hardy
Kathleen Hargis
Debra Harpole
Helen Hatton
Joseph J Heier
Melinda Hirsch
Madalena Hutcheson
Tracy Thrasher Hybl
Charlene Inglis
Les Inglis
Diane Jano
Chris & Lynne Jobe

Kathleen Kennedy
Karen Kindel
Monica Kinley-Wilson
Alma Knoll
Lisa Koehl
Maureen Koplow
Cheryl L. Kottke
Brenda Kylen
Laurie Lomillo
Diane MacIntosh
Loralei Matisse
Karen Ruth McCarthy
Susan McCauley
Karen S. McGee
Melanie McKeehan
Joan McMahon
Christopher McMurry
Lynn Mirassou
Sandra Moss
Terri Nelson-Bunge
Barbara Nozzi
Ellen Olander
Jason Paull
Jack & Sarah Peak,
    Reggie & Lucky
Sharon Pearce

Jill Richards
Kathy Riffle
Barbara Roach
Tracy Roksvaag
Claudia Rose
Cori Ruder
Maureen Schiener
Monica Schreiber
Evelyn Schwager
Leonard and Christine Seedig
Greg Suzich
Jack T. Van Skiver, Jr.
Cynthia L. Weck
Melody Welch
Sara Westgor
Lisa Wilson
Wendy Wilson
Susan Wise
Gayle Woodul
Linda York
John O Yorks III
    and Susan K. Yorks
Eileen Donohue Young
Salvatore Zingalli

Organizations:
Animal Protectors Network Puerto Rico
Avery County NC Humane Society
Boomer's Fund Beagle Rescue
Chain Free Beaufort • www.chainfreebeaufort.org
ChainFree Asheville • www.chainfreeasheville.org
Dont Bully My Breed, Inc. • www.dontbullymybreed.org
No Kill Houston • www.NoKillHouston.org
Pet Pals, Inc. • www.PetPalsInc.org
Puppy Mill Awareness Day • www.awarenessday.org
Recycled Doggies
Sunburst Foundation of Wilmington Canine Rescue

"When the Circle of Compassion Extends to ALL," an artpiece by Tamira Ci Thayne, is available from her art site. View this and more than thirty other works

Online at LittleGirlLooking.com Today!

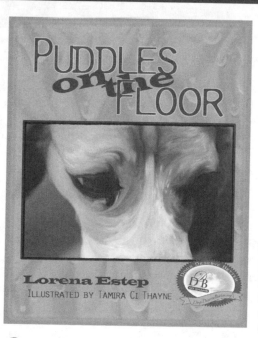

Your tireless work throughout the years has benefited so many dogs! Your new book will certainly be an asset to the rescue community and foster families as well! Best of luck to you and your new book, Tamira!

P.A.W.S. ("Providing Animals With Support") is a 501c3 non-profit charitable organization formed for the primary purpose of decreasing euthanasia rates at local shelters through spay/neuter programs, public education, and the location of quality homes for homeless animals.

Visit: P.A.W.S. Adoption Center, 859 East Tabernacle Street, St. George, Utah
Snail Mail: P.A.W.S., P.O. Box 910805, St. George, Utah 84791-0805

Phone: 435.688.9748 • Facsimile: 435.627.2105
www.dixiepaws.org • E-Mail: info@dixiepaws.org

Chain Free Beaufort
PO Box 2496, Beaufort, SC 29902
843-812-6574
www.chainfreebeaufort.org

Pet Pals, Inc.

A "True Shelter"

Located in Wyoming about 65 miles North of Cheyenne, our state capitol, we are the only licensed nonprofit animal facility in our county which covers 2,225 square miles.

Address:
Spay/Neuter Drive, Hawk Springs, Wyoming 82217
Phone 307.532.3861

A Nonprofit 501c3 Public Charity
info@petpalsinc.org • www.petpalsinc.org

Smith Virtual Office

Cherie Smith
Virtual Assistant
"Out of sight but not out of mind"
(717) 469-8481

cherie@smithvirtualoffice.com

Let me assist you in completing your to do list so you can concentrate on growing your company.

List of services:
- Book travel arrangements
- Schedule appointments with clients or colleagues
- Create PowerPoint presentations
- Transcription and proofreading
- Screen email and respond to inquires
- Order flowers, gifts, or make reservations at restaurants
- Internet research

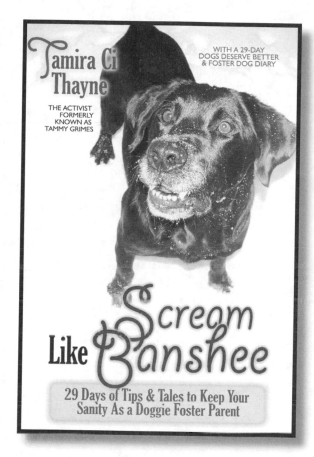

Tamira Ci Thayne

THE ACTIVIST FORMERLY KNOWN AS TAMMY GRIMES

WITH A 29-DAY DOGS DESERVE BETTER & FOSTER DOG DIARY

Scream Like Banshee

29 Days of Tips & Tales to Keep Your Sanity As a Doggie Foster Parent

From The American Dog Magazine:

Thayne, foster parent to over 100 formerly-chained dogs since forming DDB seven years ago, has sage advice and laughter for everyone from newby foster parent to frazzled do-gooder such as herself.

Scream Like Banshee includes a 29 day foster diary of Thayne's own experiences that keeps you both laughing and crying. The best part? A portion of all sales benefit her organization, Dogs Deserve Better, and bring America's dogs into the home and family. To order, visit or call:

ScreamLikeBanshee.com • 814.941.7447